Environmentalists
from our First Nations

Vincent Schilling

Second Story Press

Library and Archives Canada Cataloguing in Publication

Schilling, Vincent, 1967-
Environmentalists from our First Nations / Vincent Schilling.

(The First Nations series for young readers)
Includes bibliographical references.
ISBN 978-1-897187-98-2

1. Environmentalists—Canada—Biography—Juvenile literature.
2. Environmentalists—United States—Biography—Juvenile literature.
3. Native activists—Canada—Biography—Juvenile literature. 4. Indian
activists—United States—Biography—Juvenile literature. I. Title.
II. Series: First Nations series for young readers

GE55.S35 2011   j333.72092'397   C2011-903633-9

Printed in Canada
Co-published in the United States of America
Third Printing 2020

*Second Story Press gratefully acknowledges the support of the
Ontario Arts Council and the Canada Council for the Arts
for our publishing program. We acknowledge the financial support of
the Government of Canada through the Canada Book Fund.*

ONTARIO ARTS COUNCIL
CONSEIL DES ARTS DE L'ONTARIO
an Ontario government agency
un organisme du gouvernement de l'Ontario

Canada Council   Conseil des Arts
for the Arts   du Canada

Funded by the Government of Canada
Financé par le gouvernement du Canada | Canadä

Published by
Second Story Press
20 Maud Street, Suite 401
Toronto, ON
M5V 2M5
www.secondstorypress.ca

MIX
Paper from
responsible sources
FSC   FSC® C103567

C O N T E N T S

CHAPTER 1

Melina Laboucan-Massimo

(LUBICON LAKE BAND OF CREE)

**USES HER PASSION TO STOP OIL EXTRACTION
FROM THE TAR SANDS OF ALBERTA, CANADA**

CHAPTER 2

Winona LaDuke (WHITE EARTH BAND OF OJIBWE)

**WORKS TO RECLAIM NATIVE LANDS,
ADVOCATES RENEWABLE ENERGY RESOURCES,
AND PROTECTS NATIVE CULTURES**

CHAPTER 3

Clayton Thomas-Muller

(MATHAIS COLOMB CREE NATION)

**ADVOCATES FOR INDIGENOUS SELF-DETERMINATION
AND CAMPAIGNS AGAINST TAR SANDS EXTRACTION**

CHAPTER 4

Ben Powless (MOHAWK)

**ADDRESSES CLIMATE CHANGE ISSUES
WITH HIS YOUTHFUL ENERGY AND SKILLS**

To Kathie Hanson, Bob Holzapfel, Anna Pope, Barb Bloomfield, Jerry Hutchens, and all the other amazing folks at Book Publishing Company who have worked to make the Native Trailblazers book series a reality.

To my friend Dann Boyko, a true man of heart, who has shown me great kindness that I will always appreciate.

And to a young man who left us behind much too soon. I realize your work here was complete. Still, our hearts are with you, my Native brother and friend Summer Sky Narcomey.

A C K N O W L E D G M E N T S

Admittedly, writing the acknowledgment section is nerve-racking to say the least, because I am always concerned I am going to forget someone. In the process of creating a book, there are literally hundreds of people who help to make it happen. So if in my haste I may forget to mention someone, please let me say I am sorry and in no way was my error intentional. My appreciation is heartfelt, even if these words may not reflect it now.

A big thank you to Ben Powless for many of his photos that grace this book. Beautiful stuff!

I want to thank Delores, my wife, for her constant support of a husband who cannot ever, ever repay her for how much better my life has become since she joined me on my life's path.

I also want to thank my parents, Ray and Mary Schilling; Sharon, Mary, and Parker; Dann Boyko; Michael and Deb; Henry, Greg, Kathy, Bill, and Doris; Michael and Sylvia; and Felipe.

If there is anyone I did not mention—thanks to you, my dear friend, for all you have done to support me.

This book was certainly a process of discovery. The Native environmentalists in this book do so much to help Mother Earth, it is overwhelming. Each chapter is an attempt to show a snapshot of each of their lives; however, these stories cannot even begin to cover the magnitude of what these activists face every day while fighting for social justice, environmental reform, and a return to the ways of their ancestors.

These environmental heroes sometimes literally put themselves in harm's way to help those who cannot help themselves. Melina Laboucan-Massimo, Ben Powless, Tom Goldtooth, and others have visited parts of the world that have been torn apart by war and devastated by environmental destruction. In her fight against nuclear waste dumps, the late Grace Thorpe found herself lifted up and carried away by a group of guards during a demonstration.

Native trailblazers like Enei Begaye and Klee Benally are geniuses at organizing the masses to work for the good of Mother Earth. Their programs motivate our Native youth to take a stand and fight for what is right. It is not uncommon for the amazing individuals in this book, such as Winona LaDuke, Clayton Thomas-Muller, Sarah James, Evon Peter, and others, to be laughed at, insulted, ridiculed, and even assaulted while working for the greater good of our planet.

They have chosen a path that is not easy. They often face hardship and opposition and attacks against their characters. Yet still they press forward—but why? As many of them said to me in some form or another, they wouldn't be able to look at themselves in the mirror or be able to sleep at night if they weren't working to make a difference in this world.

I have to admit I don't envy their excruciatingly difficult road, but I am extremely impressed. These Native environmentalists are heroes who deserve to be honored in this book. I am profoundly grateful to have talked and shared some time with each one of them. I hope this book honors them in the same way that they honor our Mother Earth each and every day.

May the ancestors bless you. Aho!

Aboriginal. "Aboriginal" or "First Nations" are the terms used in Canada and throughout much of the world to refer to the Native (or original) inhabitants of the land. Aboriginal police in Canada are responsible for public order on First Nations reserves.

American Indian Movement (AIM). The American Indian Movement was founded in 1968 to bring attention to various concerns, including housing, police harassment, poverty, and treaty issues, that affect the Native communities. The organization attracts members from across the United States and Canada.

Aquifer. An aquifer is an underground layer of water-bearing gravel, rock, or sand. Water can be extracted from an aquifer using wells. Aquifers may occur at various depths; the closer they are to the surface, the more likely they are to be used for water supply and irrigation.

Atomic bomb. In 1945, during World War II, the United States dropped two atomic bombs on Japan. The first was dropped August 6 on the city of Hiroshima, killing 166,000 civilians. The second was dropped August 9 on the city of Nagasaki, killing 80,000 civilians. These two events mark the only use of atomic bombs in war.

Baby boomer. A baby boomer is someone who was born between 1946 and 1964. Baby boomers tend to think of themselves as a special generation, very different from those that came before. Their generation is among the first to grow up expecting the world to improve with time.

Boreal forest. A boreal forest is a forest of conifer trees, including Douglas firs, pines, and redwoods. Canada's boreal region covers almost 60 percent of the country's land area.

Caucus. A caucus is a group of people united to work together on a specific cause. At times a specific caucus will support a political candidate who agrees with their viewpoint or cause.

Ceremonial tobacco. Ceremonial tobacco has been used by Native people as a sacred offering for many generations. The sacred uses of tobacco differ among tribes; however, all tribes agree that tobacco should be used for healings, prayer, protection, and respect.

Colonial Williamsburg. Colonial Williamsburg is a 301-acre (122-hectare) living history museum in Virginia that reenacts life in the historic colonial settlement during the period of 1699 to 1780, when it was the center of culture, education, and government.

Colonization. Colonization refers to the movement of plantations, settler colonies, or trading posts into areas already occupied by Indigenous people. Colonialism refers to the ruling of territories and Native populations by the invading settlers.

Engineers Without Borders (EWB). Engineers Without Borders has twelve thousand members who partner with disadvantaged communities to improve their quality of life. They do this through education and engineering projects, including improved sanitation and the installation of solar collectors and wind turbines.

Environmental justice. Environmental justice is fair treatment of all people, regardless of color, gender, income, national origin, or race, with respect to the development and enforcement of environmental laws, policies, and regulations.

Environmental racism. Environmental racism is a term referring to any environmental policy or regulation that negatively affects the living conditions of or poses a health hazard to low-income or minority communities at a greater rate than wealthy communities.

Globalization. Globalization describes the process by which cultures, economies, and societies all over the world connect as a result of the Internet and other communication technologies, trade, and transportation.

Great Depression. The Great Depression was a severe worldwide economic depression that started in 1929 and lasted until the early 1940s. In the history of the United States, it is considered the longest and most widespread depression. It affected people from all walks of life and social classes.

Hau de no sau nee. In 1977 a powerful message was given by the Hau de no sau nee, also called the Iroquois Confederacy, to the non-governmental organizations (NGOs) of the United Nations in Geneva, Switzerland. The Hau de no sau nee presented three papers that gave a short analysis of Western history and called for a return to the basic consciousness of the Sacred Web of Life.

Hippie. The hippie culture was originally a youth movement that arose in the United States during the mid-1960s. It was a time of widespread tensions between generations of Americans over the Vietnam War. The advent of the hippie culture marked a change in race relations, sexual mores, women's rights, and traditional modes of authority.

Indian boarding schools. Indian boarding, or residential, schools were started in Canada in the mid-1800s and in the United States during the late 1800s to educate Native youths according to North American standards so they would fit into "mainstream" society. The children were forbidden to speak their Native languages and forced to change their identities. Punishment for breaking rules was severe. By the late 1970s, many of these schools had been closed.

Jim Thorpe. Jim Thorpe, Grace Thorpe's father, is sometimes called the greatest athlete of the twentieth century. When he was twenty-four years old, Thorpe was on the American Olympic team and traveled to Stockholm, Sweden, for the 1912 Olympics. He won gold medals in the pentathlon and the decathlon, setting records that stood for decades.

Local food movement. The local food movement is an effort to build more locally based food economies. It promotes the concept of buying locally produced food, goods, and services.

Media activism. Media activism includes publishing news on websites and creating video and audio reports to spread information about organized events and protests. Media activists provide information that is not available from traditional news agencies.

Medicine man or woman. "Medicine man" and "medicine woman" are terms used by Native American and Aboriginal peoples to describe healers and spiritual figures. Another term used for medicine man or women is "shaman."

Minority. A minority is a person who is not part of the dominant majority of the total population of a specific group. People who are minorities may have physical or cultural traits that set them apart, which may cause disapproval by the dominant majority.

National Renewable Energy Laboratory (NREL). The National Renewable Energy Laboratory was established in 1974. It is part of the US Department of Energy and is the main laboratory for renewable energy research and development.

National Wildlife Federation (NWF). The National Wildlife Federation is America's largest conservation organization. Among other efforts, NWF members work to protect and restore wildlife habitat and tackle global warming.

Nomadic people. Nomadic people move from one place to another instead of settling permanently in one location.

Nomadic hunters and gathers, like the Gwich'in, follow seasonally available wild plants and game. Nomadism is by far the oldest human way of life.

Powwow. A modern day powwow is an event where Native American and First Nations people, as well as non-Native American people, meet to dance, sing, socialize, and honor Native culture. There is usually a dancing competition with prize money awarded.

Racism. Racism is a belief that all members of a racial group have the same characteristics and that those characteristics make the group either superior or inferior to another racial group.

Recognized tribes. There are 564 tribal governments recognized by the United States government. These recognized tribes have the right of self-governance and establish legal requirements for tribal membership.

Renewable energy. Renewable energy is not subject to sharp price changes because it comes from inexhaustible sources, such as flowing water, sunshine, and wind. In contrast, supplies of fossil fuels, such as coal, natural gas, and oil, are limited. Prices for these energy sources will increase as they become scarcer.

Self-determination. Self-determination is the principle that Indigenous peoples have independent authority over their tribal lands and have the power to create tribal governments.

Shonto Begay. Father of Enei Begaye, Shonto Begay has been a professional artist since 1983. He spends his time painting and speaking to audiences of all ages. Shonto uses demonstrations and paintings to convey Native American life and how it has shaped his art.

Strip mining. Strip mining is a form of mining that involves removing a long strip of soil and rock from the surface of the earth. It is most commonly used to mine coal or tar sands. This type of mining uses some of the largest machines on earth.

Summer solstice. The summer solstice occurs on June 21 or 22 and marks the beginning of summer. The summer solstice is the day with the longest period of daylight.

Sun Dance. The Sun Dance is a spiritual ceremony practiced by a number of Native American and First Nations peoples. The ceremony includes specific dances and songs, traditional drums, the Sacred Pipe, tobacco offerings, praying, fasting and, in some cases, skin piercings on the chests or backs of the men and the arms of the women.

Sustainable development. Sustainable development is creating improvements using natural resources in a way that preserves the environment so that the needs of people can be met in the present and in the future.

Sustainable living. Sustainable living is a lifestyle aimed at reducing an individual's use of the earth's resources. Living a sustainable lifestyle means using alternative transportation and energy, eating an environmentally sustainable diet, and respecting the earth.

Tar sands. Tar sands are a combination of bitumen, clay, sand, and water. Bitumen is a sticky, tarlike form of petroleum. Methods used to extract the petroleum include open pit techniques, strip mining, and underground heating.

Vietnam War. The aim of the Vietnam War was to stop the communist takeover of Asia. United States involvement in the war lasted for twenty years. The war, however, had the support of the American people for only ten years. By 1966, youth activists began questioning and protesting the war. Unfairness, racial discrimination, poverty, and official deceit in the military draft were exposed. As the death toll and destruction from the war continued to increase, the protest movement grew and spread across the country.

Melina Laboucan-Massimo

USES HER PASSION TO STOP OIL EXTRACTION
FROM THE TAR SANDS OF ALBERTA, CANADA

Melina Laboucan-Massimo, a young woman from the Lubicon Lake Band of Cree in north-central Alberta, is a tar sands campaigner with Greenpeace Canada. She is passionate about the need to stop what the tar sands oil production is doing to the land her people have taken care of for centuries.

Melina was born in Peace River, Alberta, in 1981. She grew up in a small, isolated community deep in the forest. There were no paved roads to her community until the early 1980s, and to this day there is no running water. Her grandmother made hats, clothing, and footwear, such as moccasins or mukluks (soft boots designed for cold weather), from the hides of animals Melina's grandfather trapped. Her grandmother would line what she made with fur for warmth.

Melina's father, Billy Joe Laboucan, is a hunter and trapper who is still able to live off the land. He taught Melina respect for the earth and all its living creatures. She recalls, "When I would go with my dad hunting, I would see how he treated an animal when he took its life. I saw how he lit a fire

1

Melina Laboucan-Massimo

for it and offered the best part of the animal back to the Creator, how there was reciprocity and the need to acknowledge. You can't just take and take without there being something you give back." This knowledge formed Melina's outlook on life.

When she was in grade school, Melina went to classes in a small town outside of the reserve. Her mom was working for an addiction-counseling program and eventually became a psychologist. Melina's family headed back into the forest every chance they had. In the summers and winters they visited her grandmother, grandfather, aunts, and uncles. She always looked forward to her time in the forest, where she could see millions of stars and be reminded of just how small she was. In the forest she could hear the quiet instead of the noise pollution of the small town where they lived. These visits continued as Melina entered high school in Edmonton, the largest city in and the capital of Alberta, Canada.

In Edmonton Melina's eyes were opened to a new culture and way of life. She realized that people living in the city had lost their connection to the earth and did not see how their very survival depended on that connection. Living in Edmonton also meant confronting racism. Native people were looked down on in the 1980s, and it was considered a shameful thing to be Native. Added to that stigma was Melina's mixed-blood heritage. Her mother, Linda Massimo, is Italian, so at times Melina was not recognized as a Native. When people found out, she would hear a derogatory comment, such as, "Oh, you're Native? Why are you here, then?"

Melina did keep her sense of humor and at times joked with her friends about racism toward First Nations people. She thought it was funny that being Native became chic when moccasins came into style. She realized it was cool to be Native for a bit—and then it wasn't cool again—depending on how styles changed.

During her time in Edmonton Melina met many people from other countries who had also experienced oppression, and she formed a more global vision as a result of these contacts. She realized that many immigrants to North America did not know the history of the land or Native people. In school Melina learned a lot about the past, but she wasn't taught the true history of First Nations people. The history she did learn was full of discrepancies between what was written in the textbooks and what the reality was and is. Most of the horrific things the government did to Native people were never mentioned in public schools. Melina delved into their true history and was always educating her friends. She would ask them, "Did you know this happened? Did you know that happened?" She liked to explain that the real history of the land and Native people is hidden and kept out of the educational system.

While at the University of Alberta, Melina developed an interest in Spanish literature and took some classes in Latin American studies. She learned about the history of Nicaragua and its revolution. She drew connections between the struggles of First Nations peoples in Canada and the challenges faced by Indigenous peoples in Latin America.

Melina applied for a paid internship through the Canadian International Development Agency. The internship was part of Taking It Global, a social networking project that serves international youth primarily between the ages of thirteen and thirty. The goal of the project is to develop a more inclusive, peaceful, and sustainable world. During her internship, Melina worked on developing a teaching method that organized small groups of students to work together and learn from each other. Using the Internet and personal connections, students learned about other cultures and worldwide youth projects. Students were then able to participate in youth projects and become part of a decision-making process.

After she graduated from the university, Melina was offered a job in Brazil. She traveled to Brazil and Mexico and then went to Australia as part of an international Indigenous exchange program through which she met amazing people who influenced her life. Caring for and sharing with other Indigenous people, along with non-Native people who were striving to make changes to better their own communities, was an unforgettable experience. Altogether she traveled for seven years with her different jobs and internships.

Melina moved to Vancouver, British Columbia, on Canada's west coast and spent about four years there. She says, "I learned a lot from people in Vancouver. There were a lot of activists and artists. It is an area similar to the West Coast in the United States." Melina worked with *Redwire Magazine*, a publication that features artwork and writing by Native people. At that time it was the only such magazine in the country. *Redwire Magazine* is now available only online, but for years it was a printed magazine distributed across the country.

From Vancouver, Melina moved to Ontario to earn a master's degree in environmental studies at Toronto's York University. As a part of her studies, she researched the tar sands oil extraction process and how Indigenous peoples are affected by it. Melina discovered a number of unsettling facts about oil production and the tar sands. She realized that many people who lived in Alberta did not even know about the tar sands oil project. "It was a classic case of 'out of sight out of mind,'" she says, as people in Alberta didn't realize there had been a change from using conventional to nonconventional oil extraction processes.

The tar sands are located 250 miles (400 kilometers) north of Edmonton and cover 10 million acres (4.3 million hectares) of boreal forest. Bitumen is the thick, sticky, tarlike form of petroleum found beneath the forest. Before bitumen can be mined, all of the trees in the forest must be cut down. To turn the sticky bitumen tar into liquid fuel, an energy-intensive process involving steam injection is used. The steam-injection process uses immeasurable amounts of water and much more energy than conventional oil refining. During the process, two to four times more greenhouse gases are produced per barrel of oil than are produced from liquid oil deposits.

Melina Laboucan-Massimo

The bitumen tar deposits contain toxic substances called polycyclic aromatic hydrocarbons (PAHs), most of which cause cancer. The production of oil from tar sands releases these toxins into the water and air, consequently destroying the forests and wetlands that have supported Indigenous peoples' way of life for generations.

Oil is worth a lot of money, and the Canadian government estimates that there are 1.7 trillion barrels of oil trapped in the tar sands. Standing in the way of extracting that oil is Melina's tribe, the Lubicon Lake Band of Cree. They have never ceded their land to the government of Canada. Other First Nations peoples whose way of life depends on the land have joined their opposition to the tar sands oil extraction.

Once again First Nations people are on the front lines of an unfolding global catastrophe. Throughout history, systems called colonization and assimilation have been used to conquer Native people and force them to live like white settlers. Native people are now facing a second wave of colonization. Instead of settlers and government agencies taking their land, Native people are facing corporations and government agencies that want the natural resources under Native land. As Melina explains, "It is like saying, 'Okay, you've been living on these lands—keeping these lands pristine and in good condition—and now we are going to dig underneath them and contaminate everything around you.' It is so unjust and should not be happening."

When Melina was growing up in northern Alberta, she thought the tar sands held free-flowing oil, and she could already see the detrimental effects of harvesting this oil. Melina explains that even when Shell Oil Company arrived in the area in the 1980s, she didn't know much about the tar sands because information was not reaching local communities. She knew about the thousands of conventional oil wells that could be seen everywhere, but the tar sands sites were deeper in the forest and hidden from public view. She didn't realize what was happening until she started her own research and learned that there are three major regions of tar sands development, and more and more investment is going into the tar sands because the last reserves of free-flowing oil are drying up. Melina says, "They won't stop until they get that last dirty drop of oil."

While working on her master's degree, Melina received news that would take her back home. Her course work at the university was interesting, and her master's degree was important, but when she learned of her mother's cancer diagnosis, she wanted to be with her. She states, "It was definitely a wake-up call. I was out doing so many things. I was traveling and living in other countries, and I had been gone for seven years. I realized I needed to spend more time at home."

Even though Melina traveled back home to be with her mother, she continued her research into the tar sands. What she found was quite alarming. Her nagging suspicion was the possibility that toxins released into the environment from the tar sands mining had contributed to her mother's cancer. People, particularly those living downstream or downwind from the tar sands operations, are exposed to toxic PAHs in the air and water and by eating wild game and fish. Cancer rates in the region where her mother lived and worked were an astounding 30 percent higher than the average for the rest of Alberta. "I am not saying that is how she got cancer—you can't prove it," says Melina. "But knowing people from the community and seeing how the tar sands have affected the community—it makes me wonder."

It is not surprising that Melina questions whether her mother's cancer is related to the tar sands oil extraction. In the area downwind from the tar sands there has been a shocking increase in a number of diseases, such as rheumatoid arthritis and lupus. Also, a rare form of cancer that affects the bile duct of the liver and is typically fatal within a month after it is found has been diagnosed in three people living in Fort Chipewyan. In the general population, only about one person in one hundred thousand gets this type of bile duct cancer. In Fort Chipewyan, the occurrence is much higher: three cases have been diagnosed in a population of only twelve hundred.[1]

The effects of these toxins on wildlife are also frightening. Fish are experiencing lower reproductive rates and showing other signs of toxic stress. Animals that are trapped and hunted around the tar sands have large sores under their fur. People are afraid to eat them because of the dangers of swallowing toxins that can cause cancer. The sacred and cultural teachings of reciprocity and the practice of acknowledging the gift of a hunt, such as the traditions passed on by Billy Joe Laboucan to his daughter, are being threatened.

Melina Laboucan-Massimo

It is hard to comprehend the vast scale of destruction that has already occurred in northern Alberta. Broad swatches of conifer forests have been cleared; rivers have been polluted; and bogs, fens, and wetlands have vanished. The remaining ponds have become toxic cesspools, luring thousands of ducks to their deaths. Melina flew over some of the area with members of the Indigenous Environmental Network. She was shocked by what she saw: "It is heart-rending. You fly over and you see mines the size of cities. How can they do that? The area of destruction is so enormous it covers the entire landscape. The plan is to make the tar sands mining region about the size of Florida—which is nearly one-fourth the size of Alberta. How can our lands recover from that? You can smell the pollution in the air. It is overwhelming. I could not breathe. It was so overwhelming to see something like that. How could they want this to happen? What is going to happen in the future if this doesn't stop? People live there and depend on the land to provide what they need."

Linda Massimo's cancer diagnosis changed Melina into a dedicated tar sands activist. She applied for a position as a climate and energy campaigner with Greenpeace Canada and was accepted. She could work on the tar sands issue and still be close to her mother.

With Greenpeace, Melina found herself collaborating with non-Native coworkers on land use and environmental issues.

Although they were working toward the same goals, Melina felt that her non-Native colleagues did not have the same connection to the earth as a Native person who is descended from the original inhabitants of the area. Melina's intention is to bridge the gap between non-Native environmentalists and First Nations people, who are on the front lines of environmental destruction. Melina says, "This is something we are changing slowly, but it is definitely something that needs to happen. For true solidarity to happen, we have to have those different allies come together and work together instead of working separately."

For Melina Laboucan-Massimo, environmental activism is an ongoing commitment: "I just want to make sure there is a balance. I want to keep pushing for environmental justice and social justice. People do not have to adjust to living in contaminated areas, on contaminated land, and using contaminated water just for the benefit and profit of multinational corporations and government. We need accountability, responsible governing, and respectful understanding and communications. We need to ensure people aren't being subjected to environmental racism."

Melina says her commitment is stronger than any narrow self-interest: "If I wanted to, I could use my education and skills to 'live the good life,' for my own self-profit, but I don't think I would be happy or fulfilled. Even though the life I choose is not an easy one—I am pretty tired right now— at this point I don't think I could be doing anything else except working toward what I think should be a better place to live in. It will be nice when I'm older to say, 'I've worked for a better world for future generations.' My family had to suffer so much injustice. We have not seen justice."

Melina acknowledges the difficulties of trying to fix the great problems before us: "It is important for people to know that you can't just leave it up to a select few to make the change. The change comes from all of us. Know that you are

BE THE CHANGE!

"Be the change you want to see in the world" is a famous quote by Mahatma Gandhi. Gandhi used civil disobedience and nonviolence to resist oppression and was the popular political leader of India during the Indian Independence Movement.

just as important as anyone else and your voice is just as powerful as anyone's. It is your choice if you want to try to be that change in the world."

Melina offers advice to those who dare to make that choice: "Never feel like you're alone. There are people who have been and will always be fighting for justice. If you feel alone—just know that you are not. Empower yourself! For me it was hard, when I was younger, to feel like I had a voice. Empower yourself and know your voice is important, your voice is solid, and your voice is necessary. You are the change!"

Winona LaDuke

WORKS TO RECLAIM NATIVE LANDS, ADVOCATES RENEWABLE ENERGY RESOURCES, AND PROTECTS NATIVE CULTURES

Winona LaDuke, of the White Earth Band of Ojibwe (called *Gaa-waakabiganikaag Anishinaabeg* in the Native language) is a force to be reckoned with. She is a citizen activist who has dedicated her life to protecting the earth, advocating for renewable energy resources, and pro-tecting Native cultures. She is the executive director of Honor the Earth, founding director of the White Earth Land Recovery Project, and winner of a Reebok Human Rights Award. Winona has served on the boards of the Indigenous Women's Network and Greenpeace USA. She is an inductee into the National Wom-en's Hall of Fame in Seneca Falls, New York. In 1994 *Time* magazine named her one of the nation's fifty most promising leaders under the age of forty. In 1997 *Ms.* magazine named her

Winona LaDuke

"Woman of the Year." She is a prolific writer whose books include *Last Standing Woman, All Our Relations: Native Struggles for Land and Life, Recovering the Sacred: The Power of Naming and Claiming,* and *In the Sugarbush,* a children's book. She was the Green Party vice-presidential candidate in 1996 and 2000 but supported Democrats John Kerry in 2004 and Barack Obama in 2008.

Winona was born in East Los Angeles in 1959 to political-activist parents. Her father, Vincent LaDuke from the Anishinaabeg White Earth Reservation in Minnesota, was an actor in Western movies, and her mother, Betty, was a Russian Jew from New York who ran off with Vincent to California. Both of her parents were activists in the Native community and in the farmworkers' movement. Winona points out, "My parents were politicized already, so I was raised in a family that was pretty conscious of what was going on in the world— and we wanted to do something about it."

With a strong, supportive family structure, Winona received many valuable lessons and much advice in her life. Her stepfather, Peter Westigard, a scientist, especially encouraged her efforts. She says, "I cannot overstate the significance of his scientific discussions with me." Although she was educated in traditional schools, she also had the added influence and guidance from Native mentors Oren Lyons, Faithkeeper of the Turtle Clan of the Onondaga and Seneca Nations; Philip Deer, a Creek medicine man who traveled to Geneva, Switzerland, in 1977 as one of the twenty-one delegates presenting the Indigenous peoples' case to the United Nations; and Frank Fools Crow, a Sioux spiritual leader who helped to negotiate the end of a sixty-eight-day insurrection at Wounded Knee, South Dakota, in 1973.

When her parents separated, Winona and her mother moved to Ashland, Oregon. Her mother, Betty, became an art professor at Southern Oregon University and is known worldwide for her paintings. During the summers Winona would travel to the White Earth Reservation in Minnesota to

WOUNDED KNEE INSURRECTION AND MASSACRE

In 1973, members of the American Indian Movement (AIM) seized the town of Wounded Knee on the Pine Ridge Reservation, the site of the 1890 Wounded Knee Massacre where approximately three hundred Sioux were killed. The seizure of the site was in response to the nearly intolerable living conditions on the reservation and the violent tactics used by the tribal chairman.

spend time with her father's side of the family. They would also visit the Navajo and Hopi reservations where her dad had a lot of friends. "We trucked around a lot," as Winona puts it.

Social activism continued to play a key role in Winona's childhood. Her family was active in the civil rights movement, and in 1968 when she was nine years old, they participated in the Poor People's Campaign march on Washington, DC.

Winona's mother was an avid antiwar activist who protested against the Vietnam War. Winona remembers watching Walter Cronkite's television reports on the body counts and the bombings. When she was in the fourth and fifth grades, her mother would take her out of school for antiwar demonstrations. One time, when Winona was in the fifth grade, her mother argued with her teacher, who was a member of the Civil Air Patrol and very pro-war, explaining freedom of speech and the US Constitution. Winona's mother told him that her daughter did not have to stand and say the Pledge of Allegiance. "Mom won," Winona remembers. "I opposed the war, and I didn't say the Pledge of Allegiance in class."

Winona's lessons in social activism continued into her preteen and teenage years. In response to widespread

POOR PEOPLE'S CAMPAIGN MARCH

In early 1968 the Reverend Martin Luther King Jr. and other civil rights leaders planned a Poor People's Campaign in Washington, DC. The group demanded jobs, health care, and decent homes for the poor people in the United States. Weeks before the march was to take place, King was assassinated. The plans nevertheless continued, and on May 12, 1968, thousands of people participated in the march.

environmental destruction, the first Earth Day celebration was organized on April 22, 1970, when Winona was eleven years old. She was there, marching with her mother, as the celebration gave voice to millions of people concerned about the environment. Winona was fourteen years old when American Indian Movement (AIM) members took over the town of Wounded Knee on the Pine Ridge Reservation in South Dakota. The US Marshals Service and the FBI surrounded the town, put up a blockade, and refused entry into the town. Winona was with her father when he ran the blockade to deliver food to the Native activists.

That same year Winona joined her junior high school debate team. The topic was national energy policy. Researching for the debates taught Winona much about the mining of uranium on Navajo lands. She learned that there is no safe way to mine uranium. She says, "I retained the knowledge about energy policy, which has served me well since 1973."

Winona's school was the school to beat because it had won the state debating championship twenty-six years in a row. She was on the team until she graduated in 1976. The skills she developed on the junior high debate team have been sharpened further by her years of publicly defending Native rights and the environment. "I am not bad at debate," she admits.

Winona left Oregon at age sixteen and went to New York, where she continued her formal education. She applied for college when she turned seventeen and was accepted to three prestigious Ivy League schools: Dartmouth, Yale, and Harvard. She chose to go to Harvard.

While Winona was attending Harvard, a Cherokee representative from the International Indian Treaty Council (IITC), Jimmie Durham, came to speak on campus. The IITC brings together Indigenous people from across North and South America, the Caribbean, and the Pacific to secure independence and tribal rule. Durham asked Winona to research energy topics for the IITC. Her investigation into coal strip mining on the Northern Cheyenne Reservation in southeastern Montana revealed that the Bureau of Indian Affairs had been illegally leasing most of the land. Her research served her well when, at the age of eighteen, she represented the IITC and testified to the United Nations about human rights violations against Native peoples by the exploitation of natural resources within their territories.

After graduating from Harvard in 1982 with a bachelor's degree in rural economic development, Winona moved to her ancestral Anishinaabeg territory in northern Minnesota and founded the White Earth Land Recovery Project (WELRP). An 1867 federal treaty had promised the return of Anishinaabeg lands, but they were in reality slowly stolen and parceled out by the US government for use by the logging industry. The WELRP continues to work for the return of their original land base to the Native people, the resumption of proper land stewardship, and the development of communities, which includes strengthening their spiritual and cultural heritage.

In 1993 Winona, along with Amy Ray and Emily Saliers of the musical duo Indigo Girls, started the unique environmental

Winona LaDuke at the Indigenous Peoples Global Summin on Climate Change 2009

organization Honor the Earth. The mission of this Native-led organization is to break the geographical and political isolation of Native communities and to generate financial support for the sustainable survival of Native people. Winona continues to serve as executive director of Honor the Earth.

Winona's journey into the political arena began at a Student Environmental Action Coalition gathering of six thousand people in the Champaign-Urbana area of Illinois. Winona was pregnant with her son at the time and had her two-year-old daughter in tow. Winona was one of the scheduled speakers along with Ralph Nader, the populist attorney and activist. She had heard Nader speak at a number of events and had always considered him a "people's superhero." She recalls that first meeting with Nader: "They had me on stage with a famous writer, Harvey Wasserman, who was watching my daughter, a two-year-old, who threw up all over him.

I was really big [pregnant] and got on stage. I gave a pretty good speech. I'm pretty direct."

Winona's work in politics continued when she and other Native people attended the founding conference of the Minnesota Green Party. Acquaintances kept asking her to run for office, but she always told them she was not interested in becoming a political candidate. The turning point came in 1996 when Ralph Nader, who had become the presidential Green Party candidate, asked Winona if she would consider being included on his running-mate list. She explains, "I really respected Ralph Nader, and I thought I would be one person on a long list. A couple days later they called me and said they wanted me to be his candidate and I thought . . . jeez."

Being a candidate for vice president of the United States is a huge responsibility, so Winona had a lot to consider. When Nader said he would be honored if Winona served as his running mate, she asked, "Ralph, what does this entail?" He said, "Travel." She accepted and ran in the 1996 election. The Green Party was successful at raising environmental concerns at the national level. Winona describes her situation: "The second time I ran I was very pregnant again and Ralph approached me. I was seven months pregnant, and I said, 'Ralph, you are crazy.' I started campaigning at nine months pregnant and continued with a newborn." Winona's youngest child, Ajauwak Kapeshesit, was born in February 2000.

Her opportunities to join the vice-presidential debates in 1996 and 2000 as the Green Party candidate were thwarted by the Commission on Presidential Debates, which was run by the Democrats and the Republicans. The commission did not consider the Greens an important enough player to be included in the debates. Even though Winona had a long history of debating, she was denied access to the debate. Nearly three million Americans voted for the Nader-LaDuke ticket, and as Winona relates, "I was blamed for the election of George W. Bush—but we weren't considered factors at the time."

Today Winona continues her work for environmental justice, and the WELRP has expanded its work to end the tar sands oil extraction in northern Alberta, Canada. The WELRP raises questions about the effects the Canadian tar sands business will have inside the United States. Even though the tar sands are located in northern Alberta, some of the equipment used at the site is transported across the United States. The trucks hauling equipment to the tar sands are hugely oversized and heavy. In fact, the equipment is too heavy to carry over many Canadian roads and bridges. The plan is to bring the equipment to Portland, Oregon, transport it by barge up the Columbia River, and send it over Highway 12. This route passes through the Nez Perce Indian territory in Idaho, up through Montana, and into Alberta. The average size of one of these trucks is comparable to the Statue of Liberty lying on its side or the length of a hockey rink. To this day there have only been four loads that size on US roads, and those loads only traveled seventy-eight miles. Two hundred shipments of the oversized equipment have already been scheduled. Winona calls it "a pretty insane proposition."

These extraordinary efforts to move massive equipment are a reflection of the perceived need for oil. Winona points out: "You've got a country that is running low on oil and is entirely addicted to it. There is no plan B. They are going to really bad measures in order to feed this addiction. If you are a junkie, you do a lot of bad stuff and hang out with dealers. That is what's going on. You invade countries, and you destroy things. We are living in a junkie economy. One of the challenges we face as Native nations is entrenchment in that economy."

According to Winona everyone who is using nonrenewable resources is a part of a plan dictated to us by the big oil companies. She asks, "How about another plan? Why not envision a sustainable plan? The problem can be greatest for tribal communities. On the White Earth Reservation, for example, jobs are often fifty miles away from the homes of Native workers. That is not a sustainable or durable strategy. The question really is how do you regroup tribal economies so people don't have to travel that far to work but are still able to generate the same amount of cash? Our lifestyles need to include more local food and more local energy that would cut our energy bills."

Winona LaDuke

Developing food sustainability and the restoration of local food systems is another project promoted by the WELRP. It has developed a local business, Native Harvest, which produces and sells traditional foods, such as wild rice, hominy, buffalo sausage, fry bread mix, and chokecherry jelly.

Corn is central to the food sustainability effort, and the WELRP is trying to restore corn varieties. In the past, tens of thousands of acres of different varieties of corn were grown by Native people in the northern Minnesota region. But today seeds are unnaturally engineered and a limited number of varieties are available to North American farmers. Monsanto is a company that engineers 95 percent of all soybean and 80 percent of all corn seed grown in the United States.[1] The company's lawyers use patent infringement laws to place fines on farmers whose crops have accidentally crossed with Monsanto seeds. Farmers who plant patented seeds cannot save seeds to grow for the next harvest because they never actually own the seed they get from Monsanto; they are merely licensed to grow the crop for the company.[2]

There are significant questions about the safety of consuming genetically engineered foods and Monsanto's corn in particular. Monsanto designs its seeds to be used with other Monsanto products. The corn varieties Winona is focused on saving are heirloom varieties that have been grown by Native peoples for centuries. These corn varieties do not require petrochemical fertilizers to grow, and they are frost resistant. Winona observes, "I think that in a time of climate change, the corn could provide more food security, but our people do not even grow their own food anymore. We shop at Walmart. I am interested in changing the consciousness to a local food economy."

Using wind, solar, and other forms of alternative energy on Native land is another goal for Winona. Her aim is to reduce tribal energy consumption through conservation and the use of other renewable energy sources, such as solar energy and wind turbines. In 2002 White Earth Reservation erected their first 75-kilowatt wind turbine generator.

Winona and her team on the White Earth Reservation are developing plans to help other tribes erect wind turbines on their lands. Their plan involves linking tribal government with local municipalities, rural electrical cooperatives, utility companies, and farmers (both on the reservation and in the region).

Looking to the future, Winona says, "I think this is a life work, right there—food and energy. If I can keep to that, I can keep working in this arena."

Saving the earth and strengthening Indigenous cultures are both ongoing, multigenerational tasks. Winona is hopeful: "There are a lot of young people who have great heads on their shoulders, and I just want to keep this going."

Clayton Thomas-Muller

ADVOCATES FOR INDIGENOUS SELF-DETERMINATION AND CAMPAIGNS AGAINST TAR SANDS EXTRACTION

Clayton Thomas-Muller of the Mathais Colomb Cree Nation is an activist for Indigenous self-determination and environmental justice. He is the tar sands campaign organizer for the Indigenous Environmental Network (IEN). *Utne Reader* magazine listed him, in 2002, as one of the "thirty under-thirty visionaries" who are changing the world, saying, "When Canadian-born Cree activist Clayton Thomas-Muller performs a ceremony, the effect is both electrifying and grounding." *Yes! Magazine* hailed him as a "climate hero" in 2009. He has led several organizations,

Clayton Thomas-Muller

Tar sands

including the Indigenous and Non-Indigenous Youth Alliance (INIYA). Clayton is a board member of the innovative Collective Heritage Institute, which hosts the annual Bioneers Conference in San Rafael, California. He is also a hip-hop and rap artist and is happily married and the proud father of two sons. Clayton has done outstanding work in environmental justice and has used the hard lessons of his youth to develop the leadership skills he is recognized for today.

Clayton was born in Winnipeg, Manitoba, and first attended school there. His mother was a young, single parent from the Pukatawagan Reserve in northern Manitoba, and she moved to Winnipeg to get an education. During the summers Clayton went to the reserve to be with his great-grandparents. His mother moved often and, over time, he attended nearly forty different schools. School was hard for Clayton, although he was a gifted student and took advanced classes. He had a university reading level by the time he was in fifth grade. Things were going well until Clayton encountered a teacher who was a racist and would not respond to his request for help with his studies. Clayton remembers being ignored by the teacher, and the negative treatment he received had a profound effect on him. That was the first time Clayton failed a grade, and from then on, he gave up on school.

When Clayton was in sixth grade, his mother married a logger from Germany, whom Clayton calls "Father" to this day. The family moved to Terrace, British Columbia, where school became an increasingly difficult experience. Clayton was the first person in his family who did not go to an Indian boarding school. He was part of a new generation of First Nations kids who were put into the public school system without any support to help them adjust.

Although Clayton had experienced the racism of individuals, in high school he experienced racism in the school system. The Native curriculum that was being taught in schools always referred to Native people in the past tense, as if they no longer existed. This was a contradictory concept for Native students like Clayton who went home every day to their culture that did indeed exist.

Many First Nations people were feeling frustration and anger around this time, and this was clearly shown in the 1989 clash, known as the Oka Crisis, between the Mohawk Nation and Quebec police. The dispute began between the Mohawk and the mayor of Oka, Quebec, Jean Ouellette, over Mohawk burial grounds marked with the tombstones of their ancestors. Mayor Ouellette announced that the burial grounds would be cleared for the expansion of a members-only golf club and the building of sixty luxury condominiums. The tribe was not consulted about the plans, there was no environmental review, and all Mohawk claims to the land were denied in court. In response, Native people barricaded roads leading into the area. On July 11,

1990, on the seventy-eighth day of the barricade, a confrontation took place between the Mohawk protestors and the Sûreté du Québec, the provincial police force of Quebec. During the confrontation, police officer Corporal Marcel Lemay was shot and killed, an elderly man from Quebec died after exposure to tear gas, and another man had a fatal heart attack after a confrontation with an angry crowd of people from Quebec. The crisis ended after the city of Oka decided not to build on the land. The Mohawks dismantled their guns, threw them in a fire, ceremonially burned tobacco, and then walked away. As a result of the Oka Crisis, the First Nations Policing Policy was established by the government of Canada. The policy set up an Aboriginal police force that is responsible for public order in First Nations' territory.

Children across Canada were deeply affected when the clashes between the Mohawk and the police appeared in the national media. Clayton was in grade school when he witnessed the event on TV. He recalls, "All I was trying to do was fit in. But after Oka happened, I thought, 'You know what? I don't have to fit in.'" Kids at school taunted Clayton with racial slurs and called his mother "squaw." Clayton started getting into fights. In the midst of this troubling time, his parents divorced, and his mother moved back to Winnipeg, Manitoba. By the time he was fourteen and in eighth grade, he had failed a couple of grades. He was only fifteen when he quit going to school and moved out of his mother's house.

After Clayton left home, he started making poor choices and soon had a problem with drugs. He was incarcerated in a juvenile detention facility in British Columbia when he was sixteen years old and remained there for a year.

At first Clayton spent his time reading a lot of books and completing grades eight and nine while trying to be a model inmate. This was difficult for him, however, because Clayton witnessed the racism embedded in the detention system. He saw social workers and correctional officers encourage white kids to bully First Nations kids. In this way the white kids maintained a sort of hierarchy and control over the Native kids. Clayton and a friend successfully confronted the white bullies, and as a result, Clayton spent the last few months of his sentence shut away in the security unit. When the end of Clayton's sentence approached, he was expecting an early release for good behavior, but the authorities refused to give it to him because his parents were divorced and his mother lived out of the province. After all of his hard work maintaining good behavior, Clayton was distraught. He recalls, "It was a huge blow to my state of mind."

Instead of being released, Clayton was moved into a halfway house in Prince George, British Columbia. His attempt at good behavior didn't last long. When a corrections administrator unfairly disciplined some younger Native kids in the house, Clayton confronted her, saying, "They didn't do anything wrong." The administrator sent them back to juvenile detention anyway. Clayton spent the rest of his sentence in closed custody, which meant he was under strict supervision

Clayton Thomas-Muller

and was kept away from the other inmates. At that point, he realized, "Wow! The system is really messed up."

When Clayton was finally released from juvenile detention, he wasn't sure what to do with his life. He was sure of one thing, however: he never wanted to go to adult jail. Clayton decided to live at his mother's house in Winnipeg and go back to high school. He did well for a couple of months, but it didn't work out. He was expelled from school and was kicked out of his mom's house. Clayton found a girlfriend and got involved in a gang while trying to make sense of life. Things weren't going well, so in desperation he made a phone call to his biological father and asked for money. His father told him that if he wanted money, he should work. He gave Clayton the phone number of Clayton's older brother, Johnny, and told him to give him a call.

Clayton did call his brother, who told Clayton about his own plans to go home to the reserve and fish, hunt moose, and find a wife. Johnny told Clayton he wanted to have kids and that he planned on never leaving the reserve again. Johnny asked Clayton to give up his gang lifestyle, but he refused. Johnny pressed his argument and told Clayton he respected Clayton's manhood and intelligence, but he pointed out that Clayton wasn't using either to better himself. He stressed that Clayton's lifestyle was like a house of cards ready to fall.

At the same time, Clayton's girlfriend, who would later become his wife, was also putting the same kind of pressure on him to make positive changes in his life. She told Clayton that if he did not separate from the gang, she was going to leave him. Clayton got the message. He puts it this way: "I decided to listen. So, I gave it a try. I got away and hid." It was a good thing that he moved on when he did, because soon after there was an anti-gang crackdown in the city. As a result of that crackdown, members of his gang are in prison to this day. Clayton notes, "That could've been me."

As part of the change in his life, Clayton entered the General Educational Development (GED) life skills equivalency program called Anishinaabe Oway-Ishi, which means "Aboriginal People Leading the Way." The program is run by First Nations people and exposes inner-city youth to their culture. For the first time in his life, Clayton spent time with positive First Nations role models. He graduated from Anishinaabe Oway-Ishi as valedictorian.

After completing the Anishinaabe Oway-Ishi program, Clayton went into another program, the Medicine Fire Lodge. The program was a community-development training initiative run by the federal government for inner-city First Nations youth. Medicine Fire Lodge used a curriculum based on Native culture that taught students how to improve their communities. Students also learned about Native history, including the Indian wars in the United States and the Canadian Indian policy to remake First Nations people into people with European manners and values. The goal of the policy was to totally do away with First Nations culture. As part of that program, when Clayton was nineteen years old he attended his first Sun Dance, an important Native spiritual ceremony.

When students graduated from the Medicine Fire Lodge, they each received a $2,500 cash payment, with one stipulation: They had to create their own community initiative. Clayton developed the first Native-led community-development organization in Canada, the Aboriginal Youth Initiative (AYI). The organization existed for about four years, with Clayton as the executive director for three of them. The staff grew from two to fourteen full-time workers. The work of the AYI included political advocacy, a teen pregnancy program, gang intervention, violence intervention, and cultural and social health programs.

The success of AYI was a life-changing experience for Clayton. He had gone from being a nineteen-year-old boy making very poor choices to an executive director of a highly

Clayton Thomas-Muller

visible community organization in Winnipeg. Soon the AYI organizers had offices in four different community-development centers and in every inner-city high school. Through the AYI the Provincial First Nations Youth Council was founded. Then members of the AYI created the National First Nations Youth Council, a program of the National Congress of American Indians. Clayton found himself responsible for important programs that were making a positive difference in the lives of thousands of First Nations kids.

As if Clayton was not busy enough, while he was executive director of the AYI he was also the national youth spokesperson for the Assembly of First Nations. He helped negotiate with the government for funding that resulted in the transfer of hundreds of millions of dollars to First Nations youth programs. For that work and dedication, Clayton received an Aboriginal Youth Achievement Award.

Clayton decided to leave the AYI and enter a program at the University of Manitoba designed for individuals who never finished high school. During that time he became the head trainer for the Anishinaabe Oway-Ishi. His mornings were focused on GED-equivalency training, and his afternoons were focused on his own education.

Clayton found himself with options when he was considering career choices. He was offered a job organizing the training of Indigenous activists in South America for the Indigenous and Non-Indigenous Youth Alliance (INIYA). The job offer was a good one, and Clayton and his fiancée thought winter in South America would be a lot better than winter in Canada, so he took the job. His association with INIYA was a good fit, and he was offered a position as director of INIYA's California center. Clayton decided to take the job, and he and his girlfriend moved to California, where they were married.

While the newlyweds were living and working in California, a representative of the Indigenous Environmental Network (IEN) approached them and asked them to travel to New York City, where Clayton would help organize and prepare a delegation of Indigenous peoples attending the United Nations World Summit on Sustainable Development. The IEN staff was impressed by Clayton's ability to speak publicly and clearly explain issues. His skills in working with a variety of people in an intense environment were invaluable.

After Clayton finished the work in New York City, the couple returned to California but decided to move back to Canada. They were literally packing to move when a phone call came from Tom Goldtooth (see chapter 5), the executive director of the IEN. Tom told Clayton he was in nearby Berkeley, California, and asked to meet with him over lunch. When Clayton arrived at the restaurant, he saw Tom sitting at a table with some other Native folks. It turned out to be an impromptu interview for the position of energy and climate coordinator for the IEN. Clayton got the job and has been with the IEN ever since.

One of Clayton's first projects with the IEN was the Resisting Environmental Destruction on Indigenous Lands (REDOIL) network in Alaska. REDOIL is a statewide network of people sharing knowledge, experience, and strategies for addressing the negative environmental impact of oil and gas development. Central to REDOIL's work is the inherent right of self-determination for all Indigenous peoples and a rejection of the 1971 Alaska Native Claims Settlement Act as an unlawful violation of Indigenous peoples' control of their own land.

As Clayton continues his work with the IEN organizing communities to fight for environmental justice, he points out that both the civil rights movement and the environmental movement failed Native people. The civil rights movement did not address racism against Native people. They were also overlooked in the environmental movement when non-Native environmental concerns were assumed to be more important, even though First Nations people were the original inhabitants of the land. As Clayton explains, "These are the places our ancestors are buried. These places are our homeland. They are not empty wilderness devoid of any human contact." He points out that environmentalists are trying to

1971 ALASKA NATIVE CLAIMS SETTLEMENT ACT

The 1971 Alaska Native Claims Settlement Act extinguished Alaska Native claims to the land by transferring titles to twelve Alaska Native regional corporations and more than two hundred local village corporations. A thirteenth regional corporation was later created for Alaska Natives who no longer resided in Alaska. The members of the thirteenth corporation received only money and were not granted any land, as they didn't own land when the settlement was created.

turn Native hunting grounds and areas where traditional people harvest medicines into parks. Clayton says, "Environmental issues are fundamentally issues of human rights for Indigenous people."

Through Clayton's work with the IEN he has come to clearly understand the connection between racism and environmental justice. He works against the multinational corporations and government agencies that join forces to gain access to the oil, coal, and uranium deposits that sit under Native land. Because many Indigenous people are poor, have little legal representation, and are usually situated in isolated areas, they are disproportionately removed from their land so that large corporations can profit from the huge revenues the energy sources provide. In Clayton's opinion, this action is a continuation of the white supremacy and racism used as the basis for the forced relocation of Native people countless times throughout history. As he explains, "Removing Indigenous people from their land so that other people can acquire the natural resources contained in the land continues the practice of colonization today."

Clayton believes that Native people and all of humanity have to reevaluate our relationship with the sacredness of Mother Earth: "The sacred relationship is the one most damaged by industrialization. It is this relationship that is going to help us grab back our community and self-determination, help us heal, and help us build sustainable economies for the future."

Clayton continues, "We are walking with the prophecies. Cree people, where I'm from, have a prophecy called the 'Prophecy of the Seventh Generation.' It talks about the generation that will be born free of the colonial mind." That is what Clayton believes is happening in Canada now, where there are about two million Indigenous people out of a general population of thirty million. He predicts that before the next decade one out of every four workers will be a First Nations person. This is a tremendous shift in the political and economic power of the most powerless people in Canada. Clayton says, "That to me is a manifestation of this prophecy."

The future is full of hope and possibility. "Everything I have ever said I was going to do, I have done. I have gotten to a point in my life where I plan things out a year ahead or two years ahead and I achieve them. There is nothing that I say I am going to do that I don't do. Young people who read this book should know that the question isn't 'What can I do with my life?' It is, 'Can I handle the responsibilities of the things that I ask for?' Because no matter what you ask for—the Creator will give it to you."

Clayton wants young people to know that anything is possible. "If you are going through a lot of drama right now, it is only temporary. No matter what you visualize, you can manifest it. You just have to make sure that you are prepared.

"One of the beautiful gifts that we have as young people is that we are not tainted by politics. We are not tainted by the apathy that many of our aunts and uncles and parents are tainted by. We are still close to that innocence of our childhood, where the sky is the limit and imagination is paramount to the fact. Even teenagers are still like that. What I would say to young people is that we have every opportunity to manifest our most incredible dreams."

Ben Powless

ADDRESSES CLIMATE CHANGE ISSUES
WITH HIS YOUTHFUL ENERGY AND SKILLS

Ben Powless is a young man who has tapped into great wisdom. He describes his vision of environmental activism "as building on the ways Indigenous people are internationalized and how their social movements are focused on climate change . . . and how [they are] fundamentally changing politics and discussions at an international level." His is a vision that grew out of personal grief and social compassion.

Ben Powless was born on April 30, 1986, in Regina, Saskatchewan, where his Mohawk father worked for the Department of Indian and Northern Affairs for the Canadian government. His parents felt that the pervasive racism in Regina

Ben Powless

created a negative environment in which to raise children, so the family moved to Ottawa when Ben was young. His parents divorced in Ottawa, and Ben lived mainly with his Ojibwe mother, visiting his dad from time to time. When Ben was four years old, his mother watched him move a worm off the path and place it gently to the side. It was then that she knew she had raised him well. "My mother would always teach me ways of respecting the earth and caring for the environment," he says.

When Ben was growing up, both his parents were deeply involved in Aboriginal issues—his mother at the local level, and his dad at the national level. Ben remembers his parents always going to meetings.

Ben's mother poured her energy into working with women's shelters. Over the years, she became frustrated with the lack of understanding of the special circumstances and needs of First Nations women and their families. With the sensitivity and experience she gained from working in shelters, she went on to found the Minwaashin Lodge, a respected Aboriginal women's support center in Ottawa.

Ben spent almost every day at work with his mom at Minwaashin Lodge. He even considered it to be "a home away from home." He remembers hearing heartbreaking stories and witnessing women trying to make positive improvements in their lives. Every day he saw people helping each other. In Ben's words, "It was a very nurturing environment."

Ben's father worked with the Assembly of First Nations, a national organization representing seven hundred thousand Native people in Canada. Every three years the chiefs of the tribes in the assembly elect a national chief to be their primary spokesperson. Ben visited his dad's office frequently and spent his time there hanging out, playing, and witnessing firsthand the politics of Native leadership. He even met the national chief during one of his visits.

While Ben was growing up in Ottawa, he and his mother settled into a multiracial neighborhood of open-minded immigrant families who respected diversity. Even though his neighborhood practiced tolerance, he still felt different. White friends, who did not realize Ben was a Native person, would make racist comments and judgments. Looking back at those times, he says: "What can you do? You don't want to alienate all your friends—but you also feel you're being discriminated against. Those types of events really shaped my perceptions." There were also economic differences. Ben remembers, "Going to some of my friends' houses—they had sixty-inch-screen TVs, their parents would feed them anything they wanted to eat, they had every video game—it was strange. Growing up in my house, there were times I had to study in the bathroom because that would be the only light we had in the house. We couldn't afford cable, so we didn't watch the popular shows."

Ben's original connection to his tribal culture came from his Ojibwe mom, who took him to many local Ojibwe community events. In the late 1980s and early 1990s, a group of people opened an Aboriginal community center. The center, located on an island, was in an old, abandoned mail house that groups of tribal people had reclaimed and were living in. Ben went there quite often with his mom. For a number of years, people would cook food there and sit around the fire telling stories. Finally the government had the police shut down the center by cementing all the windows and doors to keep everyone out of the building. Ben's mother also took him to the elder's lodge, known as the "Kumik," where elders from all over the country come to express concerns, discuss problems, and serve as advisers to the Canadian government.

Both parents took Ben to various powwows. His dad took him to the Six Nations Reserve for summers and holidays, including Thanksgiving and Christmas. Six Nations is made up of the Iroquois Confederacy, which includes Cayuga, Mohawk, Oneida, Onondaga, Seneca, Tuscarora, and many other Indigenous peoples who were forced to move from their ancestral lands. Ben has fond memories of his summers and vacations at the Six Nations Reserve.

Growing up off the reserve made it hard for Ben to spend as much time with his family as he would have liked. He was only able to see his aunts, uncles, and cousins a few times a year. He missed the opportunity to be near his grandparents and hear all of their stories.

Ben considers his childhood school experiences fairly normal. In grades five and six, he realized he was good at math and was the first person in his class to finish tests. He started to read science and physics books about Einstein's theories. Ben enjoyed learning about the natural world. He was fascinated with topics that gave him a sense of new possibilities, such as time travel, the deeper levels of reality, and quantum physics. He began to draw parallels between quantum physicists and Native elders regarding their views on relativity.

After grade six, Ben changed schools and began a time of transition. The bus he rode to school could drop him off at either his dad's or mom's house. This gave Ben a chance to build a closer relationship with his dad and to begin to feel a new independence. His dad traveled quite a lot, so Ben began spending more time on his own, without adult supervision. Although this type of independence could lead to destructive choices, Ben was taught self-reliance and discipline, and he made the decision to stay away from drugs, violence, and alcohol. He had friends who shared a similar consciousness of the world and their role in it. "Thinking back," says Ben, "I was fortunate to spend time with people who shared the same sentiments as me."

High school was a time when Ben continued to develop his view of the world and his own sense of place and justice. This was also a period when Ben looked to the principles that would guide him in his professional life.

The terrorist attacks of September 11, 2001, when two planes were flown into the World Trade Center in New York

City, also shaped Ben's thinking. He shares, "For me and a lot of kids in my generation, it is hard to overemphasize how much it made people think and reflect on things that they've never thought about before. In a lot of ways, it is easy to go through school and high school and read about the world outside but not really be impacted by it. We watched TV shows and the news, and most things seemed kind of 'out there'— but when this happened, it was an awakening." Ben had a lot of Arab friends, and they used to discuss foreign policy and what should be done to change certain situations. It was the first time they really thought about these types of issues and problems and how they could be involved in the solutions.

Ben expanded his education by reading books not required in school, such as works by Noam Chomsky, a contemporary philosopher, scientist, and political activist. He read history books and came to the conclusion that the world could be understood in a lot of different ways. He also started reading about Aboriginal issues and noticed that many important events were left out of the school curriculum.

Ben's school projects in history and English began to focus on Aboriginal issues. He turned to his father for the information missing from his school textbooks. Ben's desire to learn about Aboriginal people helped him learn about his own people. His education in the ways and history of Aboriginal people began with learning about himself. Ben clarifies, "I was able to ask my father for help and asked him to explain things. I learned a lot about my history this way. This was a way for me to understand the world, to understand our people and where we came from. This was personal for me."

In twelfth grade, Ben did something that he knew would be difficult, but he also knew the experience would help him in life: he joined the debate club. The debate club was the only club Ben joined during school. He had always been shy of speaking in public, and even though he had trouble at the start of the semester, he persisted and was awarded third place at a tournament in Ottawa. The skills Ben learned

Ben Powless

boosted his confidence and honed his ability to speak in public. Ben's love of science, his exposure to the wisdom of the elders, and now public speaking—these unique interests and experiences came together to produce the environmental activist that he is today.

Also in twelfth grade, Ben developed an interest in studying physics at the university level. With the encouragement of his high school teachers, he entered the Euclid Mathematics Contest; he finished with a ranking in the upper 5 percent of those who took the exam. Based on these impressive results, the University of Waterloo in Ontario offered him a scholarship, which Ben happily accepted.

Ben had many friends in high school, but one girl in particular, Trisha, caught his attention. Ben and Trisha began dating, and before too long they fell in love. Their devotion to one another ran deep, and they decided to continue their relationship after graduation. While Ben was awarded a scholarship at the University of Waterloo, Trisha had won a scholarship to the University of Ottawa.

His first year at the University of Waterloo was not as academically fulfilling as Ben had expected; for him, there was a lot of review. Since he was a serious student, he focused on completing his work early. This gave him time to get involved in extracurricular activities. Ben's cousin, who also attended the university, was the president of the Aboriginal Student Association. She encouraged Ben to join, and he was eventually elected secretary. Before he knew it, he made a lot of friends and joined other clubs and organizations—including international aid organizations, such as Engineers Without Borders. Ben was becoming an activist. He says, "I was doing things to change the world."

Both Ben and Trisha were dedicated to their education and active at their schools, but as Ben recalls, "We were very much in love and very dedicated to each other as well." However, in March 2005, their ideal student lives changed abruptly when Trisha began experiencing pain in her legs. The doctors ran blood tests and said there was a problem in her stomach. Trisha was admitted to the hospital for surgery. When Ben got to the hospital, Trisha's parents told him the surgery was finished but that Trisha was in a coma. Things were not going well. More tests were performed, and still she remained in a coma. The doctors found that Trisha's liver was failing.

Trisha had entered the hospital on Sunday, and by Thursday her liver had stopped functioning. Still in a coma, she was flown to a transplant center in London, Ontario. On Saturday a donor liver was located, and on Sunday Trisha had a liver transplant. During surgery her heart stopped beating. On Monday, March 28, 2005, Trisha passed away. It was later learned that Trisha was born with a severe genetic disease that had poisoned her liver and her body.

"I was devastated," explains Ben. "My mom drove to pick me up and bring me back. On the way we stopped in Waterloo. I basically dropped out of the university. They were decent about it to me. I packed up all my stuff, emptied my room, and came back to Ottawa. I didn't even say good-bye to my friends. A lot of it was a blur for a while."

Ben was still dealing with grief and loss when his life took another surprising turn. A month after Trisha's death, Ben and his cousin were able to participate in an exchange program to Guatemala through the University of Waterloo. This was Ben's first trip outside of Canada.

The exchange program was directed by the university chaplain's office, and for Ben, it was an exceptional, heart-opening experience. The exchange group was able to speak with Guatemalan people who were still recovering from decades of war and repression. Ben recalls, "It was one of the most intense experiences of my life. We met government officials who lied to us. We saw churches with walls full of bullet holes. We met the victims of the civil war— widows who were still seeking the burial sites of their loved ones and former guerilla leaders who were now politicians. We visited Indigenous communities that were struggling to hold on to some of their lands. We met their spiritual leaders, who taught us about traditions and ceremonies. We traveled to about seven different cities in ten days—it was very powerful."

Along with opening his eyes to the history and struggles of Indigenous Guatemalan people, the trip helped Ben deal with his personal issue of grief. He says, "It helped me with what I was going through to see people who'd lost their loved ones."

Coming back to Canada, Ben had an expanded vision of the world that turned his understanding of life completely upside down. After his experiences in Guatemala, he knew he wanted to learn more about Latin America and other parts of the world.

Ben moved into an apartment with his dad in Ottawa and got a job with the Odawa Native Friendship Centre. The center provides a full range of programs, including food banks, programs for young mothers, and programs for Aboriginal

GUATEMALAN CIVIL WAR

The Guatemalan Civil War lasted from 1960 to 1996. It started as the Guatemalan population's response to the military takeover of the government in 1944. After the takeover, a dictator ran the government without any respect for the rights of the people. During the war, forty to fifty thousand Guatemalan citizens disappeared, and government forces killed approximately two hundred thousand people.

Finally, in 1994, after thirty-six years of civil war, a peace process was negotiated by the United Nations. National elections for president, congress, and municipal offices were held in November 1995. The civil war officially ended in December 1996, when a peace agreement was signed by government officials and leaders of the Guatemalan National Revolutionary Unity, a political party that represented the citizens of Guatemala.

men coming out of jail, among others. Ben worked in the employment training center over the summer, helping people get jobs.

During this time, Ben also visited his elders on the reserve and attended ceremonies. He visited an elder in Ottawa from his mother's side who was a professor and had traveled to Central America, Asia, and Africa. The man knew Ben and understood his desire to continue his travels. He recommended that Ben focus on world development through an exchange program between Alberta and Mexico offered by Canada World Youth. Ben sent the organization an e-mail that included his life story. He was accepted into the program and was notified that it would start in one month.

The program cost $6,000—an incredible amount of money for Ben. Fortunately, he had been saving money and had enough to make a deposit, but $3,500 more was needed. Ben put out an appeal to his friends and family for help, and in just one month he raised the rest of the money.

Ben was paired with a man from Mexico for the eight-month-long first phase of the exchange program in Alberta, Canada. The student groups developed different areas of study and created education models. Ben chose to study ways to raise funds to support programs for children.

During the phase of the program that took place in Mexico, Ben investigated political cultures by looking at social movements and Indigenous heritage. The intent of the program was to create ways to develop appropriate programs that work, and to expose the programs that do not work or are even detrimental to people. Ben recalls, "The biggest conclusion I came away with was that to do any sort of good

Ben Powless

work, you have to start with your own community. You have to be able to start at home."

After the Canada World Youth program ended in 2006, Ben went back to Ottawa with a clear sense of purpose and direction. He became involved with a number of different organizations and got a summer job with the Youth Environmental Network. Ben's main task was to help plan a youth conference for September 2006 that would bring together Aboriginal groups, labor unions, and student and youth groups from across the country. Together the participants decided to focus on climate change. The conference was Ben's initial experience with environmental issues, and it was the birth of the Canadian Youth Climate Coalition.

Ben began organizing monthly climate change actions on the local level. The Canadian Youth Climate Coalition was a vehicle for moving the public dialogue about climate change into mainstream Canada. Within a year, climate change became the number one concern of the Canadian public.

Ben resumed his studies, this time enrolling at Carleton University with a clear sense of where he wanted to go with his education. The school allowed Ben to tailor an education that would prepare him for the direction he wanted to take in life. His focus is on human rights, Indigenous course work, and environmental studies. He is currently finishing up his undergraduate thesis.

In 2007 Ben contacted the Indigenous Environmental Network (IEN) and connected with activist Clayton Thomas-Muller, a member of the IEN staff (see chapter 3). Ben was looking for a mentor to help him become more educated about environmental activism, and Clayton's many years of experience were an incredible help.

Even though there was a lot going on in Ben's life, he couldn't pass up his next opportunity. The Canadian Youth Climate Coalition joined forces with the Canadian Coalition for the United Nations Educational, Scientific, and Cultural Organization (UNESCO), a youth advisory group composed of leaders

CLIMATE CHANGE

"Climate change" refers to any noticeable change in climate over an extended period of time, such as changes in rainfall, snowfall, temperature, or wind. We can see the effects of climate change when sea levels rise, glaciers shrink, trees bloom earlier, growing seasons get longer, rivers ice over, lakes freeze later and break up earlier, permafrost thaws, and the range and distribution of animals and plants change.

Natural factors that affect the earth's climate include the sun's intensity and slow changes in the earth's orbit around the sun, but human activities also play a role. Cutting down the earth's forests, expanding cities, and burning fossil fuels are a few examples of human activities that trigger climate change. When fossil fuels, such as coal and oil, are burned, concentrations of greenhouse gases increase in the earth's atmosphere. These gases prevent heat from escaping to space, somewhat like the glass panels of a greenhouse.

Greenhouse gases keep the planet's surface warmer than it otherwise would be, and as these gases continue to increase in the atmosphere, the earth's temperature climbs. The eight warmest years on record (since 1850) have all occurred since 1998, with the warmest year being 2005. Most of the warming in recent decades is very likely the result of human activities.[1]

from different organizations across the country. As part of a summit they were sponsoring, Ben was asked to be a representative in Mexico. At the summit, Ben was in meetings for five days learning how to plan action strategies. He says, "I remember coming back to Ottawa and taking everything in with fresh eyes after having been influenced by the culture of Mexico."

In November 2007, Ben was offered a position with the IEN, and a few months later he was asked to travel to Indonesia for two weeks to attend the United Nations Climate Change Conference. He could hardly believe this was happening. The conference was held during exam time, so he had to take time away from his studies to participate. Although his professors had the power to say no, they were very understanding. "One of my professors was actually jealous," Ben says, "because he wanted to go."

Ben Powless

Ben traveled to Bali, Indonesia, and met with twenty other youth delegates working on climate change issues, but that was just the beginning of his travels. He became more involved with the IEN, and he traveled to Peru for a conference on Native peoples. He explains, "I ended up in the Amazon as a journalist and photographer, covering a story on how the Indigenous people were trying to stop oil and mining companies from coming into their communities, coming into the Amazon waters, or cutting down their trees. Ever since then I have been involved with that community."

What is next for Ben Powless? He says, "One of my crazy dreams right now is to work and save up money so that I can buy a motorcycle and go on a trip starting in North America and driving down to Latin America, visiting different Indigenous communities—many of which are involved in the struggles to protect their lands, their culture, their language, and their rights—as a way to document what's going on in the world at a political level, and how we can work together and share."

Ben continues to work with the IEN, representing the organization at various international events, most recently at the High-Level Conference on World Food Security, Climate Change, and Bioenergy, which was held under the auspices of the United Nations Food and Agriculture Organization. Ben has solid advice for young people: "I really would have to say to follow your heart and follow whatever wisdom is given to you, especially by your elders. That is a huge reason for what I am today. I would also like to stress the importance of getting an education. You cannot understand the doors that will open to you until you have gotten it. There is no doubt as to the number of places that you can go to get an education as well. Those things should be capitalized on. Learning our language is an education. Learning about our culture is an education. We have to be able to engage and accept the responsibility for these things."

Tom Goldtooth

FIGHTS FOR ENVIRONMENTAL AND ECONOMIC JUSTICE, SUSTAINABLE DEVELOPMENT, AND EFFECTIVE ECONOMIC SYSTEMS

Tom Goldtooth is the executive director of the Indigenous Environmental Network (IEN), a Native-based non-governmental organization (NGO) focused on environmental and economic justice. The IEN works with communities and individuals, locally and globally, to protect sacred sites and the environment by organizing direct action campaigns and building alliances with like-minded groups. According to its website, the IEN was formed out of a love of Mother Earth and a desire to heal the wounds inflicted by "the collective greed of humanity." The organization started in 1990 during a national gathering of young people and older leaders who met to discuss the environmental assaults on their lands and communities. Tom

Tom Goldtooth

Goldtooth joined the IEN a year later, but his journey began long before that.

Tom grew up in Arizona on the Navajo reservation near the remote areas of Marble Canyon and Vermillion Cliffs, along the Colorado River. Both Navajo and Dakota, he is known as Mato Awanyankapi, which means "The Bears Look Over Me" in the Dakota language. Tom's mother is Diné (Navajo). Through example she gave him a strong sense of the importance of education. His mother was the first Navajo and the first Native woman to receive a college degree in microbiology. She became a medical technologist and later ran laboratories at large hospitals, both on and off the reservation. Tom's stepfather was a Navajo policeman and a rancher who raised cattle, horses, and sheep.

The largest town near Tom's reservation was Page, Arizona. The town sprang up in 1957 as a housing camp for workers who were building the Glen Canyon Dam in a gorge of the Colorado River. The water that backed up behind the dam formed Lake Powell, where Tom loved to swim when he was young. He also hiked and camped in the mountains of the Kaibab National Forest on the north rim of the Grand Canyon.

While growing up, Tom spent summers with his grandparents, caring for his grandmother's sheep. His grandfather was a well-known medicine man, and many people came to him for help. Both of his grandparents influenced his life by instilling an ethic to work hard, respect the land, and always take care of his family and community.

As a youth, Tom attended spiritual ceremonies that profoundly influenced his character. The Sacred Pipe, a ceremonial object that is part of Tom's Dakota heritage, was used to pray to the Great Spirit and to receive messages and guidance. Tom's family was a Sun Dance family, and each year he attended a Sun Dance. This important religious ceremony of the Plains Indians is usually held annually by each tribe at the time of the summer solstice.

Tom Goldtooth

A Lakota holy man, Pete Catches Sr. from the Pine Ridge Reservation in South Dakota, also influenced Tom on his spiritual journey. He taught Tom to work hard, to remember the many gifts that Mother Earth offers us, and to always offer prayers and thanks to the Creator and Mother Earth. Ceremonies still are an important part of Tom's life. He carries the knowledge he gained from ceremonies and uses it in his work today. As he explains, "Ceremonies help me in the work I do helping our Native communities address environmental justice issues."

Tom attended public school in Page, where racism was not yet an issue. Half the students were Navajo and the rest were white children whose parents had moved to Page to build the dam. Navajo and non-Navajo residents worked together in the small town without much conflict. Conditions were different, however, in the larger reservation border towns, such as Flagstaff, Arizona, and Farmington,

New Mexico, where white people had reputations for saying disrespectful things to Navajo people. Later, in the 1970s and '80s, white people in Farmington beat some Navajo people, killing some of them.

Tom's early life was one of cultural isolation. His one window to the outside world was a rock-and-roll radio station that broadcast a show by popular disc jockey Wolfman Jack, who drew upon his love of horror movies to create a raspy-voiced, howling on-air persona. Tom grew up listening to heavy metal, Motown, The Beatles, the Rolling Stones, and Jimi Hendrix, who was part Native American.

Tom was born in the 1950s and was part of the baby-boomer generation, which experienced a modern life that was very different than the traditional culture of his elders. He relates, "I grew up in a time when many of my generation, as youth, had to search for answers on how to survive in a changing world and changing environment."

After high school Tom's life took some interesting turns. He entered an engineering program at Arizona State University in Tempe, but after a couple of years he quit college and joined the US Army. He served for three years as a finance and accounting specialist, keeping track of troop payroll and travel expenses. He later became an instructor in the US Army Race Relations Department, helping military personnel understand the issues of racism and human relations in the armed forces.

While stationed at Fort Lewis, Washington, Tom helped form a group of Native soldiers, many of whom were returning from Vietnam, to socialize and network together. The group later helped provide protection and security to the nearby Nisqually Indian Tribe, whose members were experiencing racism and conflicts over fishing rights. The tribe reserved the right to fish, hunt, and gather shellfish from treaties they made with the US government in the mid-1850s. When tribal members tried to fish and hunt off their reservation, however, they were arrested for violating state law.

After his discharge from the military, Tom stayed in Washington, in the Puget Sound area. He attended Tacoma Community College and earned a degree in human services. He later attended Pacific Lutheran University in Tacoma, where he studied social work. His goal was to learn skills that could help him support the culture and values of Native families and communities.

With his formal education completed, Tom moved to the Navajo reservation and took a job as the director of a regional tribal social services program. He had a staff of thirty people who served Navajo communities and addressed issues concerning domestic and sexual abuse.

Next he moved to Minnesota to become executive director of the American Indian Family Center, in Saint Paul. There he developed the Back to Mother Earth project, which created opportunities for Native families in Saint Paul to spend weekends in the country. Participants learned cultural skills, such as building Native lodges, planting traditional crops, and tanning hides. They also had the opportunity to attend sweat lodge ceremonies.

In 1991 Tom took a job directing the solid waste program for the Red Lake Nation in northern Minnesota. This move put him closer to his wife's people, the Ojibwe. His job was to close three landfills that were operating open and burn dumps. At this time, burning garbage was the normal practice in America's heartland, for both county and reservation areas. Then the US Environmental Protection Agency (EPA) found that this practice contributed to air pollution, so they set stricter management standards and began closing open and burn dumps. With the new standards in place, landfill issues became very important in the United States.

During this time environmental protection was a fairly new idea in the United States. "Not in My Backyard" became a popular slogan used by east coast residents who did not want toxic dumps, incinerators, or landfills near where they lived. Many cities, communities, and townships had political clout

Tom Goldtooth

and put pressure on the private waste industries to find other places for toxic landfills. This is when environmental racism came into play. Tom explains, "The industries went to areas and communities that did not have a lot of political power—areas where people of color lived and Native communities, including Native reservations."

Red Lake, an area precious to the culture of the Ojibwe people, was targeted for dumping toxic waste. Through his role with the tribe, Tom became part of the Minnesota governor's task force on solid waste. He met with the solid waste officers of different counties who were also trying to address the issues of landfill management. He found county governments had much more money, political clout, and access to engineering experts than the tribes.

Tom learned that in EPA Region Five, which included Illinois, Indiana, Michigan, Minnesota, Ohio, Wisconsin, and thirty-five Native American tribes, all the tribes were trying to address toxic waste and solid waste management issues. He also learned that there were not enough resources available to the tribes. Tom could see the racism and lack of infrastructure the tribes were experiencing. He believed the EPA and the federal government failed both to live up to treaty rights and their responsibilities to protect Native lands and future generations of Native people. He was able to address this issue as environmental injustice and reminded the EPA, the Bureau of Indian Affairs, and the Indian Health Service that they all had the responsibility to protect Indian country and to address issues of environmental racism and environmental injustice. Tom knew that tribes throughout the country needed funds to develop effective environmental protection programs on their reservations.

At the same time, Tom also worked in Red Lake to educate the Ojibwe people. They were not very knowledgeable about how many toxins were in the average household's wastewater. By talking to elders Tom tried to develop resources and ways for the people of Red Lake to protect the lake's water and secure the environment.

While Tom was developing a vision and a personal track record for protecting the environment in Indian country, his friend and clan sister, Winona LaDuke (see chapter 2) encouraged him to attend the first National People of Color Environmental Leadership Summit. The goal of the summit was to bring together people of color and examine their basic civil and human rights in their fight for environmental and economic justice. Tom wondered if the gathering would have much importance for him since he worked at the local community level and not the national level. Winona thought that Tom's environmental justice concerns needed to be part of the summit. As Tom puts it, "She convinced me to go to this event."

It was a good move. The summit, which was held in Washington, DC, in October of 1991, was a historic event that acknowledged and made known the concept of environmental justice. About eighty Native representatives from tribes across Canada and the United States attended. Wilma Mankiller, who had just won a landslide re-election as principal chief of the Cherokee Nation, was there, as was Saint Regis Mohawk Tribe Environmental Specialist David Arquette. Grassroots organizers against Peabody Coal Company at Black Mesa, Arizona, showed up, along with traditional people from many cultures. Tom was moved by the dedication of the people who were part of the summit. He recalls, "What really got to me was that these grassroots

Tom Goldtooth

people came with their stuff packed in cardboard boxes and knapsacks, and they really cared about the protection of Mother Earth."

The summit attendees quickly developed a Native peoples caucus and, because of Tom's work experience and familiarity with the issues, the caucus elected him as a spokesperson. He recalls, "It was the grandmothers and the sisters and brothers who were there that really got to my heart—talking about, literally, life and death issues. People were experiencing cancer from the years of uranium mining, people from the coal power plant regions were dying from respiratory illness. I also heard testimony from Mexican American people who were dying from the agriculture industry due to pesticides and the lack of washing facilities and African American people from the southeast who had been around the chemical-polluting industries along the Mississippi River corridor from Baton Rouge to New Orleans."

Tom began to see the level of danger and the immense size of the problem: "This is what hit me really hard at that summit. I think this is what really locked it down for me that I need to do something. This is a big issue. This is a crisis. We made a commitment as Native people at the summit that we will stand with our brothers, including African American, Asian American, Latino, and poor white folks; we will stand together to confront environmental racism and demand solutions and action. But we also said, 'We will stand with you if you also support our treaty rights, because this is a treaty rights issue as well. We share something, which is environmental racism and environmental issues.' And we said, 'We are also different, we are your older brothers and sisters on this continent—we have treaty rights and issues that we are confronting—will you stand with us?' And they made a commitment to stand with us."

The following year, the IEN recruited Tom. For several years he was able to work with both the Red Lake Nation and the IEN, which asked him to help Native organizations and develop networks so Native people throughout the United States and Canada could have a voice in environmental protection. Tom worked on this project until 1996, when he decided to end his employment with the Red Lake Nation so he could work full time with the IEN.

The IEN's work is far reaching. The organization helps tribes by using clear language when explaining issues so that people can understand them. The IEN also provides tribal leaders with detailed information regarding the federal government's environmental protection plans and their obligations to tribes. In addition, the IEN works with communities that are dealing with toxic waste dumping in landfills, and it also has a mining program designed to inform and protect people in areas affected by mineral extraction.

The IEN has influence not only in local politics but it also contributes to US policy by developing methods for environmental protection in Indian country. The organization raises funds to get community representatives to national government meetings so they can try to change policy.

The IEN brings together Indigenous people from impoverished nations and remote areas around the world who are experiencing the same conflicts and even interacting with some of the same companies that the IEN is confronting in the United States. This has brought Tom into an international role as he works for the voice of Indigenous people to be heard. As he explains for all Native people, "We feel like we've been waiting for five hundred years."

Also on a global level, the IEN is protecting biological diversity and endangered species by helping the United Nations (UN) establish protocols for trading and selling traditional seeds and medicinal knowledge. The IEN is also involved with the UN on the issue of persistent organic pollutants (POPs), chemical substances that exist in the environment and pose a risk of causing adverse effects to human health and the environment. The UN had worked for many years to develop a treaty limiting and reducing POPs, such as polychlorinated biphenyls (PCBs), dioxin, and others. To keep the treaty-making process moving forward, the IEN networked with Indigenous people around the world.

Working with the UN on the issue of POPs was one of IEN's first campaigns. In addition, the IEN partnered with Greenpeace United States to produce *Drumbeat for Mother Earth*. This documentary film explains how POPs contaminate the traditional food web, violate treaty rights, travel long distances, and are passed from one generation to the next during pregnancy, causing health problems such as cancer and learning disabilities. *Drumbeat for Mother Earth* brought Tom into the world of media and video production. The film also brought his empowered Native voice to an international audience.

In addition to his commitment to environmental justice, Tom works to find solutions for sustainable development and appropriate economic systems that respect Native val-

Tom Goldtooth

ues. He feels traditional languages are integral to that value system. He believes that for Native people to be able to overcome doubt and fear of failure, they must value the original instructions and teachings that incorporate and reinforce the importance of Native language. Tom explains, "You talk about environmental protection? It reminds us that we have a language that defines our relationship to the environment, whether it is our relationship to the trees, plants, medicines, soil, air, or water; that definition comes through the use of our language. Many of our tribes say parts of their language cannot be interpreted into English. If we only have English, and not our Native language, then we don't have the Native words defining our relationship to the land. This work has reminded me of the importance of culture and language.

"We are all environmentalists because of the teachings, which come through our Native culture and language, of how we are supposed to act and be as Native people. The youth need to be able to reach out to their elders and maintain that language. That gives us the courage to stand up and protect our homelands and to provide a safe environment for our future generations. It is important when we talk to the younger generation of Native Americans to tell them that we have values and culture and the deepest respect for the sacredness of Mother Earth. That is interwoven with our language and knowing our history, because it is within the history of our tribes that we have teachings, and we have the original instructions on how to live in a harmonious balance with our Mother Earth as well as with our community and all life. That is why I have said, 'Native Americans are the original environmentalists.'"

Tom has particular advice for young men: "Looking at protecting Mother Earth, there is a female quality and essence that we have to look at. There is the importance of the sacredness of that female creative principle—looking at Mother Earth, in particular, also challenges us to look at our own values and how and what our relationship is to our sisters and our moms and our grandmothers and our daughters and our nieces. As men, especially if we are to protect the sacredness of Mother Earth, then that also defines how we protect women within our own families and communities and our circle."

When speaking about his work for environmental justice, Tom is realistic: "Everyone needs to know what he or she is getting into when approaching these problems. This work is tough; it is not for the weakhearted. It takes its toll on family. I have to travel a lot, but my kids understand. They are older now, and sometimes they are able to travel with me, but it is hard work, working for the survival of this planet. It's tough work."

Grace Thorpe

DEDICATED HER RETIREMENT YEARS TO KEEPING NATIVE RESERVATIONS FROM BECOMING NUCLEAR WASTE DUMPS

Grace Thorpe, of the Sac and Fox Nation, was the daughter of Olympic gold-medal winner Jim Thorpe and an activist for Native rights before the word "activist" became popular. Her work began during the takeover of Alcatraz Island in 1969, and for the remainder of her life she continued to advocate for Indigenous rights and the return of Native lands. Today Grace Thorpe is best known for her tireless work to keep reservations from becoming nuclear waste dumps.

Born in Yale, Oklahoma, on December 10, 1921, Grace was a tribal member of the Sac and Fox. She was a descendant of Chief Black Hawk, a great warrior and leader in the Black Hawk War of 1832. Her Native name was NoTen O Quah, which translates as "Woman of the Power of the Wind that Blows Up Before a Storm" or "Wind Woman."

Her father, Jim Thorpe, was the legendary athlete who won gold medals in the pentathlon and decathlon in the 1912 Olympics. It took some time and a lot of effort, but Grace eventually convinced the International Olympic Committee to return the two gold medals that were stripped from him because he had played semiprofessional baseball.

Grace Thorpe

Grace was one of seven children. She was the young-est of her mother's three daughters, plus she gained four half-brothers when her father remarried. Grace's father and mother divorced when she was four years old. That same year Grace was sent to the Chilocco Indian School, a board-ing school in north-central Oklahoma.

Founded in 1884, Chilocco was one of many federal schools designed to dissolve tribal identity and erase Indig-enous beliefs and practices. The large school, which was not on a reservation, housed up to nine hundred students, used military discipline, and stressed instruction in trades and manual and domestic labor, which were referred to as "actual work." The students received government-issue uni-forms, scanty meals, and inadequate health care. Students endured twenty-two bugle calls a day until 1930, when the practice was ended. Although Grace was away from her fam-ily, she admitted she had some happy times at the boarding school. Despite tribal rivalries and language differences, the students were knit together by bonds of loyalty and love.

During World War II Grace joined the Women's Army Corps and served as a corporal. She was stationed in New Guinea, a large island north of Australia, and was there in August 1945 when the United States dropped two atomic bombs on the Japanese cities Hiroshima and Nagasaki. The destruction was phenomenal. A few days after the second bomb, the Japanese surrendered. At first Grace was elated with the atomic bomb and the Japanese surrender. "We were all delighted," she remembered. "We blew jeep horns and whistles. We were told it stopped the war."

A few months later Grace arrived in Japan and served on the staff of General Douglas MacArthur, commander of the US forces in the Far East. When Grace saw the devastation from the bombings, along with the cancers and genetic deformities caused by the radioactive fallout, she no longer felt excited about how the war ended. The devastating images of atomic bomb damage would stay with her for the rest of her life and cause her to take action against nuclear waste.

While in Japan, Grace met and married Fred Seeley and had two children, Dagmar and Thorpe. They returned to the United States and settled in Pearl River, New York, in the 1950s. She and Fred eventually divorced. After her children grew up and went to college, Grace moved to California.

Grace was forty-eight years old and living in San Francisco when she became involved with a group called Indians of All Tribes. Many members were Native people who were living in San Francisco because of the relocation program and termination policy (see sidebars, pages 62 and 63). The Urban Indian Relocation Program encouraged American Indians to move away from reservations and into certain cities. The Bureau of Indian Affairs estimates that from 1952 to 1967, 200,000 American Indians were lured to cities, including San Francisco, with the promise of a better

URBAN INDIAN RELOCATION PROGRAM

In 1952 the federal government began the Urban Indian Relocation Program. The purpose was to remove Native people from reservations to seven major urban cities where jobs were supposedly plentiful. Relocation offices were set up in Chicago, Cincinnati, Cleveland, Dallas, Denver, Los Angeles, San Francisco, San Jose, and St. Louis. Bureau of Indian Affairs employees were supposed to orient new arrivals and manage financial and job training programs for them.

The people who relocated were given money to tide them over. The amount of money given was determined by family size; for example, a man, his wife, and four children got $80 a week for four weeks. Many people did not receive the help they needed.

It is estimated that as many as 750,000 Native Americans migrated to these cities between 1950 and 1980. The 2000 US Census shows that 64 percent of Native Americans lived in cities, compared to 8 percent in 1940.

life. The Indian Removal Act of 1830, in contrast, forced only 89,000 people off their ancestral lands (see sidebar, page 63).

As part of relocation, the Bureau of Indian Affairs promised resettlement aid and job training. People were given one-way bus tickets to relocation cities, but many had inadequate housing and remained unemployed for months. At the same time that the relocation program was put into effect, the government's termination policy sought to end the federal recognition of tribes, effectively nullifying treaties made more than a century earlier with tribal nations.

TERMINATION POLICY

In 1953 the US Congress announced the federal policy of Indian termination. Congress passed termination acts on a tribe-by-tribe basis. From 1953 to 1964, the government stopped recognizing 109 tribes and bands as sovereign dependent nations. The number of Native Americans who gave up tribal affiliation totaled over 12,000, or 3 percent of the total Indian population. Approximately 2.5 million acres of land held in trust for tribes was removed from protected status during these years.

Because of these programs and policies, the poverty on reservations, and the hopelessness felt by Native Americans, many Indigenous people were beginning to think that it was time to speak out and bring awareness to their plight. Then, in October 1969, the San Francisco Indian Center, a gathering place for displaced urban Indians, burned down. Native people in the Bay Area needed a new home, and

INDIAN REMOVAL ACT

In 1830 President Andrew Jackson pushed legislation called the Indian Removal Act through both houses of Congress. It gave the president the power to negotiate removal treaties with Indian tribes. The southeastern tribes did not want to give up their lands, so Jackson used military action to make them leave. This forced relocation is known as the Trail of Tears.

they focused on Alcatraz Island, which had once been the rocky site of a federal prison. A group called Indians of All Tribes was formed, and they planned the nonviolent action to occupy Alcatraz Island. The group wanted the occupation to be a positive example of Native people working together; their hope was that the action would bring a sense of pride back to Native Americans.

This was not the first attempt to occupy the island. The US government abandoned Alcatraz in 1963 and handed it over to the General Services Administration, which then rejected several proposals from Native groups regarding the island's use. So on March 8, 1964, a small group of Sioux attempted to take the island, using the 1868 Treaty of Fort Laramie as justification. The treaty promised the Sioux surplus federal land, but it was clear that the Sioux had no ancestral claims as far west as San Francisco. The group, singing and drumming, lasted only a few hours on the island before US Marshals ushered them off peacefully. Their action was unsuccessful, but the seed of an idea had been planted. The possibility of reclaiming Alcatraz as Indian land stuck in the minds of many.

Early in the morning on November 20, 1969, seventy-nine American Indians, including Grace Thorpe, sailed to Alcatraz and began the occupation. This bold action electrified Native people across the continent. Young people from more than fifty tribes rallied on Alcatraz throughout November. By the end of the month, they were six hundred strong.

Indians of All Tribes issued a written proclamation declaring, "We Hold the Rock!" The gathered tribes offered to purchase Alcatraz with glass beads and red cloth, the items Europeans had bartered in exchange for the island of Manhattan. As the occupation stretched into weeks and months, life became harder for the activists. Some said they could feel the spirits of prisoners still locked in their prison cells. Then Yvonne Oakes, the thirteen-year-old stepdaughter of Richard

Oaks, a Mohawk spokesperson for the group, fell to her death from a third-story balcony. The family was devastated and left the island.

To pressure the demonstrators, the federal government cut off phone service, electricity, and the water supply. Grace Thorpe negotiated with the government to ensure the health and safety of the occupants. She managed to secure a power generator, a water barge to deliver fresh water, and ambulance service. For the most part, demonstrators relied on their own resources, although they had widespread community support. Grace's devotion to the struggle was unreserved. She said, "Alcatraz made me put my furniture in storage and spend my life savings."

The conditions on Alcatraz deteriorated when the government withdrew the water barge. Food began to run out as well. On June 11, 1971, US Marshals, FBI agents, and the Coast Guard invaded the island and physically removed all the Native people who were inhabiting Alcatraz. The occupation, which had lasted for nineteen months, came to an end. (Read more about the Alcatraz occupation in chapter 7.)

The international notoriety achieved by the Alcatraz occupation inspired Indigenous activists around the globe. The occupation also resulted in US government policy changes related to Native Americans. Ten major policy and law shifts included the passage of the Indian Self-Determination and Education Assistance Act; revision of the Johnson-O'Malley Act, which called for better education for Native people; passage of the Indian Financing Act; passage of the Indian Health Care Improvement Act; and creation of a new government post, assistant interior secretary for Indian affairs. During the occupation President Nixon quietly signed papers rescinding termination, the policy designed to end federal recognition of tribes. That was a major victory for all Native Americans, and many attributed it to the determination and self-sacrifice of Indians of All Nations.

Grace Thorpe continued to be an activist after Alcatraz and helped many tribes with land reclamation and media relations. She became involved in a land dispute between the Pit River Tribe, the federal government, and the Pacific Gas and Electric Company (PG&E). During the dispute, Native protestors camped out on PG&E land in Shasta County in northeastern California in an attempt to seize an area roughly the size of Connecticut. The Indian Claims Commission had already given ownership of the land to the Pit River Tribe in 1853. However, the land was later taken away illegally by the creation of a federal law.

In a clash involving riot police, federal marshals, and police dogs, nearly a dozen officers physically removed Grace Thorpe and the other protestors from the property. The Pit River Tribe was offered $29 million for the land, but the tribe said the land held cultural value that could not be priced. Eventually much of the land was returned to them, and the tribe received a monetary payment for land that was not returned.

In the early 1970s, Grace served as the press connection for the Fort Lawton, Washington, occupation. As a result of this action, the activists secured land for the Daybreak Star Cultural Center, an urban base for Native people in the Seattle area. Grace was also the press connection when activists occupied an abandoned 640-acre military communications base near Davis, California. As a result of this occupation, the Deganawidah-Quetzalcoatl University, the first university for Native American and Hispanic students in the United States, was established on surplus land.

In 1971 Grace Thorpe moved to Washington, DC, where she attended school and earned a paralegal certificate from the Antioch School of Law. She joined the National Congress of American Indians (NCAI), the largest Native American civil rights organization in the United States. While with the NCAI, Grace focused on persuading companies to build factories on reservations to provide work for underemployed Native residents.

In 1974 she was hired as a legislative assistant for the US Senate Subcommittee on Indian Affairs and served for two years in the House of Representatives on the Indian Policy Review Commission. Grace then continued her education and received a bachelor's degree in Indian law from the University of Tennessee at Knoxville in 1980, when she was fifty-nine years old.

In that same year, Grace returned to the Sac and Fox Reservation in Oklahoma and earned a master's degree in business administration at the Northeastern State University at Tahlequah. Using her experience and education, Grace served as a district court judge for the Five Tribes (Cherokee, Chickasaw, Choctaw, Creek, and Seminole) of Oklahoma. She also served as the health commissioner for the tribes. Grace had the ability to be successful in many areas because of her broad-based education.

Grace was in her sixties and a happy grandmother when a new threat forced her back into action. In 1991, while reading a newspaper article, she learned that the Department of Energy had distributed applications to store toxic nuclear waste to every state, municipality, and Indian tribe in the country. According to Grace, not one state in the United States wanted the waste, and only three counties were considering taking it. In contrast, twenty-one Indian tribes expressed interest. Grace's Sac and Fox Tribe was one.

In a recorded telephone interview with Alpha Institute, a group that provides communication resources to Native Americans, Grace said: "When my tribe put in for this nuclear waste study grant, it brought back all those memories of what I had seen in Nagasaki when I was in Japan. I knew this was not the kind of thing my tribe should get involved in, or any Indian tribes, or anybody."

Sac and Fox leaders argued that the tribe needed the money; payment for storing the waste was projected to be in the millions of dollars. Grace countered that there is no way to safely dispose of deadly radioactive waste. It would take hundreds of thousands of years for the radioactivity to diminish. So Grace put together a petition against storing nuclear waste on the reservation, and she went door-to-door collecting signatures and talking to tribal members about the dangers of radiation poisoning. She worked tirelessly to bring the issue to a vote. Due to her efforts, the tribal community refused to store toxic nuclear waste on the reservation. Respecting the desires of the people, the Sac and Fox tribal council withdrew its application.

Grace founded the National Environmental Coalition of Native Americans (NECONA) in 1993 to warn other tribes

◆

GRACE THORPE'S SPEECH TO THE NATIONAL CONGRESS OF AMERICAN INDIANS

December 1, 1993, Sparks, Nevada

The nuclear waste issue is causing American Indians to make serious environmental and possibly genocidal decisions regarding the future of our people. What to do with the nuclear wastes produced by commercial and military reactors has stumped the minds of the most brilliant scientists and physicists since the advent of the atom bomb nearly fifty years ago. No safe method has yet been found for the disposal of the most lethal poison known in the history of man.

What kind of society permits the manufacture of products that cannot be safely disposed of? Shouldn't we have a basic law of the land that prohibits the production of anything we cannot safely dispose of?

It is wrong to say that it is natural that we, as Native Americans, should accept radioactive waste on our lands, as the US Department of Energy has said. It is a perversion of our beliefs and an insult to our intelligence to say that we are "natural stewards" of about the danger of storing nuclear waste. The organization encourages tribes to proclaim their reservations nuclear-free zones. The group's efforts have successfully created seventy-five nuclear-free zones, and many tribes have withdrawn applications for nuclear waste zoning.

Today, many cities, towns, and communities worldwide have declared themselves nuclear-free; however, New Zealand is the only country that has antinuclear laws written in its national legislation. In addition to nuclear-free zones, there are now nuclear-weapon-free zones that prohibit the stationing, testing, use, and development of nuclear weapons

these wastes. The real intent of the US government and the nuclear industry is to get rid of this extremely hazardous garbage on Indian lands so they can go and generate more of it. They are poisoning the earth for short-term financial profit. They try to flatter us about our ability as "earth stewards." They tell us, when our non-Indian neighbors object to living near substances that will be poisonous for thousands of years, that this is an issue of "sovereignty." It is not! It is an issue of the earth's preservation and our survival.

Perhaps we should ask ourselves a few questions about the motivation of our new friends from the nuclear industry. Is nuclear technology being offered to us because the US government and corporations think we got a raw deal in the past and now they want to make it up to us by giving us this wonderful opportunity? Or is it because they are being run out of town on a rail in the rest of North America and now they are turning to us?

I would like to invite you to consider expressing your sovereign national rights in a different way by joining a growing number of tribal governments that are choosing to declare their lands nuclear-free zones.

inside a particular state, region, or area. The United Nations General Assembly has called the zones a positive step toward nuclear disarmament.

On September 26, 1999, Grace received the internationally recognized Nuclear-Free Future Award. She specifically received the Resistance Award for founding NECONA. In 2003 the Oklahoma Indian Affairs Commission honored her at the Native American Heritage Celebration Day at the Oklahoma State Capitol.

Grace never stopped lobbying against the spread of nuclear waste storage on Native lands. After a lifetime of helping many Native people and encouraging tribes to make their reservations nuclear-free zones, the much-loved Grace Thorpe passed away on April 1, 2008, at the age of eighty-six.

Sarah James

DEFENDS THE PORCUPINE CARIBOU HERD AND THE ARCTIC NATIONAL WILDLIFE REFUGE IN NORTHERN ALASKA

S arah James is from the far reaches of the Arctic Circle, but her voice reaches around the world. As a dynamic spokesperson for the Gwich'in Nation and a board member of the International Indian Treaty Council, she is a forceful opponent of oil drilling in the Arctic National Wildlife Refuge (ANWR). When asked what made her decide to become an environmentalist, Sarah answers, "I don't know if I would say 'I became'—that is the Western way. It is not up to me. It is up to the Creator. I grew up with it and probably will die with it. That is how we are as Indian people. That is the responsibility the Creator gave to us. To be environmentalists, that is our responsibility."

Sarah grew up in one of the most isolated communities in Alaska, Arctic Village. She was raised in the traditional Gwich'in way, speaking Athabascan and living off the land. Her family, which included two brothers and a sister, was out on the land most of the time. They always did everything together. Her parents were traditional people and, like most Gwich'in, had a personal relationship with the environment. Sarah's father was a trapper and her mother was a craftsperson. Her mother made the family's boots, coats,

Sarah James

gloves, and mittens. She also tanned skins and prepared foods. The entire family would pick berries so Sarah's mother could make delicious jams. Her mother taught Sarah how to do everything she could do. Both parents taught their children all they knew about the land as well as sharing and storytelling. It was a good life.

Sarah recalls, "My mother did a lot of beading to sell. She made fur parkas. She did this to raise money. My dad would make a trip to town. A plane would come out sometimes and would land in the lake or river. It would have to be planned and paid for."

When Sarah was growing up Arctic Village was very small; at times, fewer than fifty people lived there. Her family also had a cabin on the Salmon River, where their nearest neighbor was fifty miles (eighty kilometers) away. Sarah's family traveled up the river in a boat with an outboard motor.

Until the 1950s, the Gwich'in lived mostly a nomadic lifestyle, fishing, hunting, and gathering through northeastern

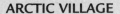

ARCTIC VILLAGE

Arctic Village is a Native American community one hundred miles north of Fort Yukon, Alaska. The population is 152. The village is located in the large Gwich'in-speaking region, where more than 95 percent of the community speaks and understands the Athabascan language.

Alaska and western Canada. For Sarah's family, this changed when new education laws forced the family to stop living the nomadic life. Sarah recalls the effects of the new mandatory-education laws: "This is what colonized us to begin with. The government was saying, 'Living on the land is not good enough. You must have a European-based education.'" Her parents were in partial agreement with the government and told Sarah to get an education so she could one day get a good job and have a good life. They, however, continued to live off the land.

The government said there were not enough children to start a school in Arctic Village. The closest town with a school was Fort Yukon, and Sarah's family moved there in 1950, when she was about seven years old. Sarah and her siblings were enrolled in school for about three years, but she hardly ever attended. The school was far from their home, and it was too cold to walk. One day her brother got into trouble at school. When that happened, her mother said, "This is not the place for my kids." So the family went back to Salmon River.

Sarah's mother wanted to restart the village at Salmon River, but not enough people could live there. Every family had the same problem with the government and the mandatory-education laws. Government officials eventually came and told Sarah's parents that they had to stay in one place and put their children in school. They were told that if they did not comply, their children would be put up for adoption. So Sarah went to school off and on for years. She never could complete a full year, however, because her family continually needed to go back to the land to survive. When Sarah was thirteen years old, she still didn't know how to speak English.

Sarah attended a number of different boarding schools. During her time away from her family, she yearned to return home, but her parents were forced to follow the demands of the government.

One of the boarding schools Sarah attended was the Chemawa Indian School in Salem, Oregon. When she boarded the Greyhound bus to travel to her new school, she thought of the trip as an adventure. Too soon she learned the adventure would not last. The school required students to make major adjustments to fit into white society. Indian children were placed in boarding schools away from their families so that they would be far from Native influences. The goal was to make them more like white people. Sarah remembers, "I had no choice. In order to make it in life, you had to be like them. You had to wear their style clothes."

Sarah recalls the greed and the waste that were all around her at the boarding schools. There was food, yet the students were hungry all the time. They were fed government commodity foods, which the schools got for free. These foods, which were high in fat, salt, and sugar, made the students fat.

While living and going to school in Salem, Sarah felt racism against Indians. One time when she was on the street, a lady walked up to her and said, "Why are you window-shopping? You can't afford it."

Life at school was not easy. Sarah had to study whenever she had a chance. She also had to work to afford the things she needed for school. For example, during her senior year, she was determined to buy a senior gown and yearbook. So she worked on weekends. During the week, all she did

CHEMAWA INDIAN SCHOOL

The Chemawa Indian School opened in 1880 and is still operating today. It is the oldest continuously operating boarding school in the United States and has graduated thousands of students.

was study from the time she got up until she went to bed. In 1967 Sarah passed her high school degree requirements and graduated when she was twenty-one years old.

After graduation Sarah was relocated to the San Francisco Bay Area in California as part of the Urban Indian Relocation Program. The program was designed to move people from reservations to seven major cities where jobs were supposedly plentiful. As part of the relocation program, Sarah was given help finding a place to live. She also enrolled in a business college and was required to pass the program in six months. She was told that after she completed the program she would be given help finding a job.

People from the relocation program did find Sarah a job in an insurance company, but she barely made enough money to get by. She was living from paycheck to paycheck. In addition, she had to move a lot because of the prejudice against Indian people. Despite the fact that Sarah found it tough to live in the city, the late 1960s was a fascinating time to be in San Francisco. Sarah began hanging out on Haight-Ashbury Street, the center of the hippie culture. She witnessed many protests about issues she was interested in.

A large number of Native Americans were living in the San Francisco Bay Area because of the Urban Indian Relocation Program. Sarah began spending time with Native students enrolled at San Francisco State University. The students were studying Indian law and were trying to figure out how to draw attention to injustices toward Native Americans. Under the leadership of Richard Oakes, a Mohawk and instructor at San Francisco State, the group formed Indians of All Tribes. In what turned out to be a turning point for Indigenous peoples' sovereignty issues, they decided to reclaim Alcatraz Island, the site of an abandoned federal prison in the middle of San Francisco Bay. On November 9, 1969, seventy-five Native Americans landed on Alcatraz Island and declared it sovereign Native land. By the end of the month, more than six hundred young Native people from more than fifty tribes occupied the island.

Sarah was a part of the Alcatraz occupation. She and the other young people who were seizing Alcatraz felt fully justified because Indians from many tribes, including the Apache, Modoc, and Paiute, had been imprisoned on the island, and many died there.

Many members of one tribe, the Hopi, were subjected to murder and enslavement in Arizona and then sent to Alcatraz for rejecting forced education and refusing to farm the way the US government demanded. As Sarah summarizes, "They first tried to use Native American people as slaves. Native American people would refuse to work, so they took them out to Alcatraz Island. At that point they just called it 'The Rock,' and it is still called 'The Rock' today. A lot of people don't realize that a lot of our people died on that island. There is the dungeon where they huddled together and chanted—that is where they gathered driftwood and got fires going. That is how some of them survived. People want to use that rock for ceremonial purposes. Many of the Native prisoners who died there never got blessed. That is why we want the land back." (Read more about the Alcatraz Island occupation in chapter 6.)

Sarah's father died during the time of the Alcatraz occupation, and Sarah moved back to Arctic Village. The area was still isolated. There was no electricity, and most of the residents practiced a seasonal subsistence lifestyle. By this time, Sarah had a son. She was a single mother after ending an eight-year relationship with her son's father.

Returning to the Arctic with her son renewed Sarah's pride in her people and their history. The Gwich'in once numbered about one hundred thousand; however, a significant percentage of the population died from the diseases introduced by Europeans. Now there are only about eight thousand Gwich'in living in northeast Alaska in the United States and in the Yukon and Northwest Territories in Canada. Despite the border between the countries, the Gwich'in are one nation of people. The Gwich'in used to be a nomadic people, who moved and gathered when there were good harvests. They would stay together for the winter, but because they moved so often, they were unable to create a permanent village. Today there are fifteen villages in the Gwich'in Nation.

Life for the Gwich'in changed with the arrival of the Europeans in the late 1600s. French trappers were the first to enter Gwich'in territory. Before then, it is said that the

2005 Peace March

birds were plentiful and so loud the people had to yell at each other to be heard. But a few years after French trappers arrived, the bird population was reduced by half. The trappers used a poison called strychnine for their bait, and any animal that ate it died.

There was a time of great weakening of the Gwich'in Nation. The loss of game led to hunger and then starvation. Old World diseases, such as chicken pox, the flu, measles, and tuberculosis, invaded and spread. Indigenous people had no immunity against them. Famines and epidemics killed thousands.

In 1905 help came to the Gwich'in from an unexpected source—an adventurous Episcopal archdeacon from London named Hudson Stuck. Stuck was traveling and stopped in Fort Yukon at the trading post, where he saw Gwich'in orphans whom he called "good-looking people." He realized the Gwich'in were a strong people, but that they were dying. He decided something had to be done, so he asked the government for assistance. The government, however, never answered his letters. So he turned to his supporters and started a mission for orphans and a hospital. As a result, he saved many Gwich'in lives.

Later, John Fredson, who was a young Gwich'in dog handler in Stuck's expedition, was instrumental in securing the Gwich'in homeland. After finishing high school, Fredson traveled to the southern United States, where he attended college and graduated from the University of the South in Sewanee, Tennessee. He returned to Yukon Village in 1937, the same year Congress passed the Indian Reorganization Act. Fredson's education gave him the background to understand how the law could be used to secure the homeland of the Gwich'in people. The new act allowed Indians to create reservations and tribal governments to interface with the US government.

Fredson began an educational campaign to prepare the Gwich'in for signing the agreement offered by the Indian Reorganization Act. He traveled by canoe and dog sled to fishing camps and isolated communities of hunters and trappers.

INDIAN REORGANIZATION ACT

The US Congress passed the Indian Reorganization Act in 1937. The act gave certain rights to Native Americans, including Alaska Natives, by returning to Native Americans the management of their assets (mainly land). The act included provisions intended to create an economic foundation for people living on reservations. To get the rights being offered, a tribe had to sign on with a majority vote of its members within one year of the effective date of the act.

Fredson surveyed the boundaries of a reservation as directed by the Gwich'in people, compiled their signatures, and filed the paperwork with the Department of the Interior. In 1938, as a result of Fredson's efforts, the Gwich'in were awarded 1.8 million acres of land under the Indian Reorganization Act. In 1945, when he was around fifty years old, Fredson died of pneumonia. Some Gwich'in say he was as important to their people as George Washington was to Americans.

Fredson could not have foreseen the threat to the Gwich'in homeland that Sarah is now confronting. Billions of barrels of oil lie under the frozen sands of the Porcupine caribou calving grounds, and the oil companies want that oil. In 1988 the Gwich'in Steering Committee was formed to oppose oil drilling and to protect the herd, whose meat sustains the Gwich'in through winter and into the springtime. The Gwich'in people consider themselves the caribou people. Because they are dependent on caribou meat for their existence, the fate of the Gwich'in has been tied to the fate of the caribou. If the herds diminish, the Gwich'in would be forced to replace caribou meat with store-bought meat. The cost to an already struggling, isolated culture would be disastrous.

ARCTIC NATIONAL WILDLIFE REFUGE

The Arctic National Wildlife Refuge (ANWR) in northeastern Alaska covers more than 19 million acres (nearly 8 million hectares). It is the largest national wildlife refuge in the United States. The northern coast of the refuge provides habitat for migratory water birds, including ducks, geese, shorebirds, and swans. Coastal lands and sea ice are used by caribou, who seek relief from biting insects during the summer, and by polar bears, who hunt seals and give birth during the winter.

Gwich'in creation stories describe how the caribou has a piece of Gwich'in heart in its heart, and each Gwich'in has a piece of caribou heart in his heart. It is a sacred biological contract. The people protect the caribou, and the caribou provide the people with what they need. Even in times of famine, the Gwich'in would never hunt or disturb the caribou in their calving grounds on the North Slope of what is today the ANWR. Biologists estimate that forty thousand calves are born there each year. The Gwich'in call this land the "sacred place where life begins."

Why is the coastal plane of the ANWR crucial to the survival of the Porcupine caribou herd? As spring vegetation appears on the coastal plain of the refuge, blood-sucking insects plague pregnant caribou and young claves. Both mosquitoes and black flies keep the caribou from feeding and their calves from nursing. The tiny predators even cause the caribou to run around, act distracted and crazy, and injure themselves. When there is no wind, the caribou must move constantly to avoid the insects. The coastal plain offers breezes and cooler temperatures that limit the insects' assaults. The cold winds provide an environment in which the caribou can rest and get the food necessary for their survival.

To the Gwich'in, the caribou have a value beyond any price. Caribou meat is an important staple in the Gwich'in diet. Without the protected coastal plains, the caribou herds would shrink. The caribou and the Gwich'in face ruin if the oil industry gains access to the remaining untouched 5 percent of the North Slope. The oil companies want access to the area, but Sarah and the Gwich'in Steering Committee are defiant. Sarah says, "Maybe there are too few of us to matter. Maybe people think Indians are not important enough to consider in making their energy decisions. But it's my people who are threatened by this development. We are the ones who have everything to lose."

The thirty-year record of the multinational oil corporations in Alaska does not bode well for the ANWR. British Petroleum (BP), Conoco, Exxon, and other oil companies have turned more than one thousand square miles of Alaska's North Slope into an industrialized oil field. Each year there are, on average, five hundred reported spills of petroleum products and other toxic substances inside that zone.

The National Academy of Sciences study titled "Cumulative Environmental Effects of Oil and Gas Activities on Alaska's North Slope" concluded that oil development harmed the environment and Indigenous people in many ways. While noting significant effects on caribou, grizzly bears, polar bears, shorebirds, waterfowl, and endangered bowhead whales, the report singled out the Porcupine caribou herd as being the most vulnerable to human-caused stresses of all the caribou herds in Alaska. This is the very herd the Gwich'in depend on. The study concluded, "It is unlikely that the most disturbed habitat on the North Slope will ever be restored."

The push to drill for oil on the ANWR and the calving grounds demanded a strong response from the Gwich'in. Sarah understood this was a critical time. She and the tribal

ALASKAN PIPELINE

In 1968 oil was discovered on the North Shore of Prudhoe Bay, Alaska. The area was found to be the richest oil field in the United States. A pipeline was constructed from the North Slope to the nearest port, extending almost eight hundred miles (thirteen hundred kilometers) to the south. The pipeline crossed many miles of Native land. In 1971, with major petroleum dollars on the line, the Alaska Native Claims Settlement Act was signed into law. Native tribes relinquished Aboriginal claims to their lands in exchange for access to 44 million acres (nearly 18 million hectares) of land and a cash payment of $963 million. The settlement was divided among thirteen regional, urban, and village corporations, which managed the funds.

elders brought the Gwich'in people together to take a position against oil and gas development. In June 1988, Arctic Village became the site of a great meeting of the entire Gwich'in people, the first such meeting in more than one hundred years. The gathered elders and spiritual leaders chose Sarah to be the spokesperson for protecting the caribou.

Some people would like to believe that adding the ANWR oil to the world's supply would reduce prices at the pump, but it is quite possible that the reverse may be true. In the past, increases in oil supplies have been offset by decreases in production by oil-rich nations, which kept gas prices high at the pump. The United States possesses only 3 percent of the world's known oil reserves, including ANWR, but consumes 25 percent of the world's oil production. Reduction of oil consumption and a move to renewable energy sources makes more sense.

Hopes by some that the oil industry would provide meaningful, well-paying jobs for Indigenous people have not panned out. Studies by the National Academy of Sciences, the North Slope Borough, and the Alaska Department of Labor report that few local residents are directly employed by the oil industry. The workforce, which is occasionally hostile to Native people, remains largely white. The jobs that are offered to Indians are often menial or token. The National Academy of Sciences asserts that the oil industry has not improved Native people's quality of life: "The stress of integrating a new way of life with generations of traditional teachings has increased alcoholism, drug abuse, and child abuse. Higher consumption of nonsubsistence food has increased the incidence of diabetes."

So far, plans for oil drilling have met opposition. While the oil industry describes the targeted coastal plain as a small portion of the refuge, conservationists describe the coastal plain as the most environmentally important and sensitive area of ANWR. The pro-drilling lobby talks about the small "footprint" the drilling pads would make. However, the oil-drilling sites are scattered throughout the drilling area, and each site requires

Sarah James

power plants, utility lines, water reservoirs, airstrips, helicopter pads, equipment sheds, and living quarters. In addition, all of these sites need to be connected with a web of roads and pipelines. Oil industry spokespeople suggest the roads could be built and used in the coldest times of the year on a bed of man-made ice. The US Fish and Wildlife Service point out the flaws in this argument, noting that the caribou calving area has only enough usable water for ten miles of ice roads. All additional water would be drawn from surface ponds and lakes. Lowering their levels would mean that the water would completely freeze in winter, killing off the fish that help hold the mosquitoes and flies in check during other seasons. The industry is considering other alternatives, such as bringing in vast amounts of water to the area or constructing permanent gravel roads along with gravel pits and landfills.

To Sarah, the truth of the matter is obvious: "The oil companies keep saying that all their roads and pipelines aren't going to bother the caribou. But we know the caribou. We know they don't like all that stuff, especially when they are having their calves. We are concerned about all the salt and chemicals they put on their roads. It can drain onto the tundra, get into the water, and be unhealthy for young caribou. A report from the Canadian government tells us that the caribou have already been disturbed around the oil fields. If we lose the caribou, there will be no more—forever."

The Gwich'in and their environmentalist allies have held the line against the oil companies for now. However, the drive for oil—and the profits made from it—remains a constant threat.

Sarah has clear advice for students and young people, especially Native people, growing up today: "Anybody can be a caretaker of the land, not just Indigenous people, but that is what we live like because we know that is our responsibility. That is our duty. That is what we are born for, and that is what we are going to die for. We need to stand our ground."

CHAPTER 8

Enei Begaye and Evon Peter

WORK AS A COUPLE ON ENVIRONMENTAL ISSUES AND SUSTAINABLE STRATEGIES FOR NATIVE PEOPLE

Enei Begaye Peter and Evon Peter grew up thousands of miles apart, but both had the same devotion to their communities: Enei to the Navajo in Arizona and Evon to the Gwich'in in Alaska. They also shared a devotion to the environment and worked to defend it from harm. Ultimately, these shared traits brought Enei and Evon together.

Enei and Evon met while preparing for the World Summit on Sustainable Development, also known as Earth Summit 2002, in Johannesburg, South Africa. The United Nations organized the summit to bring together leaders from business and non-governmental organizations (NGOs). Both Enei and Evon were part of a delegation organized and led by the Indigenous Environmental Network.

The two first spoke by phone when the delegates organized the trip to South Africa. Their first face-to-face meeting happened at a Youth for Environmental Sanity (YES!) conference, where delegates discussed strategies and solutions for

Enei Begaye and Evon Peter

sustainability in their own communities. Evon first saw Enei in a group setting. Everyone was sitting in a circle, taking turns introducing themselves. When it was Evon's turn, he stood up and said, "My name is Evon Peter. I am a chief from a small remote tribe in Alaska with no running water or electricity. I am looking for a woman to be my wife, who is also good at administration." Everyone had a good laugh.

Enei was watching Evon closely while he introduced himself. She suspected he was only half-joking about finding a wife who was good at administration. Enei recalls thinking: "Oh jeez, who is this guy? He's kind of cute, but I wonder what fool he'll get to do that. Good luck with that one, buddy!"

Evon remembers seeing Enei and hoping to meet her. As part of a game designed to help them all get to know each other, the attendees each put their name in a hat and picked a name out of the hat. They then became that person's secret angel. For the next six days of the conference, the secret angel did nice things for the other person. The fun part of the game was that no one knew who his or her secret angel was. As Evon recalls, "I told myself, if I pick Enei's name, I am going to marry her." When the hat came around, lo and behold, he pulled out Enei's name. Evon thought, "Oh, man, I wonder if I was serious when I said that in my mind?"

A couple days into the conference, Evon decided to write a poem for Enei that read: "Beauty will be the way, love will keep us together, and the stars will be our guide." Later, Enei told Evon that her secret angel wrote her a poem that was pretty intense. She did not realize Evon was her secret angel! The two of them spent the rest of the conference hanging out together. They looked forward to the World Summit on Sustainable Development, where they would spend more time together. Evon says, "We ended up in South Africa a few weeks after that. I felt like we were really meant to be together."

Enei and Evon were chosen to attend the World Summit because they were working for sustainability in their communities. They recognized this shared commitment, and their love and respect for one another grew. They realized they could do a lot of good if they worked together, and they knew they could be a strong team. A year later they were married, but the marriage came at a cost. Both partners were closely tied to their communities, and being together would require sacrifice. Ultimately, they agreed to spend time in both Alaska and Arizona. Since Evon was the Gwich'in chief, Enei decided to move to the Arctic Village when they married. After their first daughter was born, Evon resigned from being chief and they moved back to Enei's homeland in Arizona.

One of their first collaborations as a married couple was starting an organization called Native Movement. The group's goal is to inspire and support young Indigenous leaders with culturally based leadership development and sustainability programs. Native Movement offers sponsorship and technical assistance for Indigenous organizations and initiatives across North America. The organization has two main branches: the Indigenous Leadership Institute in Fairbanks, Alaska, and the Native Movement Southwest in Flagstaff, Arizona.

Events in Evon's childhood were not always ideal; however, because of his strong Gwich'in ties and his mother's guidance and example, Evon made positive choices that led him to where he is today. The lessons he learned in life are the basis of the ideals he lives by.

Evon's parents married when his father was quite a lot older than his mother. His father was Jewish and his mother is Gwich'in. His parents moved to Israel, where their first child, a daughter, was born. Their plan was to live in Israel, but after his father suffered a nervous breakdown, they moved to Los Angeles, California, where Evon and his brother were born.

Life in Los Angeles was not perfect, and Evon's mother missed her Gwich'in people. She decided to take her three young children back to Arctic Village. Evon's dad followed his wife and family to Alaska, but life in such isolation was difficult for him. After one year, Evon's father moved back to Los Angeles and his parents divorced.

Evon's mother, Adeline, was then a single parent. The family had no running water, and they didn't get electricity until Evon was ten years old. Adeline was strongly grounded in the traditional ways of her Gwich'in community. Since Evon was her oldest son, she felt he should be raised traditionally. Evon speaks with admiration about his mother: "She is probably one of the most knowledgeable Gwich'in people alive today as far as history and general knowledge about our people."

When Evon was ten years old, his father died. Their relationship had grown distant, so his father's death did not make a difference in Evon's life. Evon attended school in Arctic Village with only seven other students. Most of the time, not all the students showed up for school. Luckily for Evon, the school had two computers and he was the only student interested in them. He had a lot of time to mess around on the computers and learn what they could do.

When Evon was twelve and in junior high, his mom decided to move the family to the South Cushman area of Fairbanks, Alaska. When his family lived in Arctic Village, Evon learned a lot about the Gwich'in traditional way of life, but his formal education was lacking. As a result, the switch to a large public school in his new neighborhood was difficult.

His family's situation was also challenging. They lived in low-income housing, along with all the black, Hispanic, and Native people in the area. There was a lot of drug dealing in South Cushman. Evon recalls that when he was thirteen, he was taken out of class with eleven other Native students and told by school officials: "There are higher odds of you guys being dead, in jail, or a high school dropout by the time you're twenty-five than there are of you finishing high school." Evon also remembers that the officials were correct. Out of the twelve students, one committed suicide and the rest dropped out of school. As Evon says, "We contributed to the school officials' statistics."

Evon was a rebellious teenager, and even though he was in an honors program, he decided to drop out of high school. He didn't discuss his decision with his mother; he just gave her the paperwork to sign. Adeline was always supportive of her son, but she asked him what his plan was. Evon told her, "I am going to go to work for a while, and then I am going to go to college." His mom replied, "Good plan."

Evon stuck with his decisions and made adjustments when necessary. He was having trouble finding a college program that would accept him because he didn't have a high school diploma. Finally, one of the acceptance officers at the University of Alaska in Fairbanks said, "Evon, if you put

Evon Peter

as much work into college classes as you do coming in to argue with us every week, you'll probably be able to make it through college."

The university was willing to admit Evon, but first he had to get his general equivalency diploma (GED), certifying that he had high school–level academic skills. He was given a practice college entrance exam, and he scored five points higher than the average high school student entering college. After performing well on that test, he was allowed to take regular college courses.

Evon's future was looking positive, but he realized he had issues that he needed to deal with. As a child growing up in rough neighborhoods, he had suffered abuse. He knew he couldn't change all of his problems and bad habits overnight, so he started working on a plan. He decided, "In five years I am going to quit smoking cigarettes. In ten years I am going to work through a lot of the deeper issues."

Some powerful dreams he had as a teenager influenced the direction Evon was taking in life. Discussing the details of dreams is unthinkable in the Gwich'in culture, however, so he never talked to anyone about them. Still, he knew the dreams had shown him who he was and what he was capable of doing. At age seventeen, he realized he wanted to be a good father, and he knew he could choose to do the right thing. As Evon explains, "I made a commitment to live my life on a path where I would challenge myself to grow and do things to fulfill whatever roles are there for me to fulfill." Today Evon is a committed father and husband.

While at the University of Alaska, Evon designed a class he called "Native Alaska Leadership." The Native Studies Department approved the class and gave Evon college credit to travel around Alaska to meet with chiefs from various tribal communities and gather information. The Native leaders and chiefs invited him to tribal gatherings so he could see firsthand how tribes were managed. When Evon spoke at the gatherings, other attendees, including newspaper and television reporters, found him to be a clear spokesman for Native issues. They began seeking him out.

When he was twenty-one and about to graduate from college, Evon received a job offer to run a rural university center in Fort Yukon, Alaska. The university hired him despite the fact that the position required six years of administrative experience and a master's degree. His job at Fort Yukon was to find funding and write grants, increase enrollment, and help students adjust to university life.

After working one and a half years as an administrator, Evon met Chief Peter John, an Athabascan elder who lived to be 102 years old. Chief Peter John recognized Evon's potential and bestowed a chief's necklace upon him in a traditional ceremony. Six months later, the Gwich'in elected Evon chief. He was only twenty-four and very young for a chief, so he had to learn fast. The first year was especially hard, he remembers: "There were times I would be out debating big government officials in Anchorage, and I would have to go to the bathroom because so much pressure built up in me that blood would start running out of my nose." Evon would get the bleeding to stop and go right back into the meeting.

Evon became a strong defender of the caribou, who were threatened by oil drilling and global warming. He wrote, "My ancestors are the oldest inhabitants of the Americas. If the caribou go away, our whole tradition and our culture will change, and the next generation will be lost. The protection of this area became a fight that consumed not only my people but also my own life from the time I was very young."

As Evon was growing up in the distant north of Alaska, Enei was growing up far to the south in Arizona. Both were members of tribes that faced environmental battles with large energy companies. Evon's ancestral lands are situated over oil reserves, and Enei's ancestral lands over coal. The companies wanted these resources.

CHIEF PETER JOHN

Chief Peter John was born in 1900 in central Alaska. When he was growing up, there were almost no white people in the area. In those days, his tribe still sometimes hunted moose with bow and arrow and bear with spears.

His mother died when he was two years old, and when he was a teenager his father died. John was then on his own. For one summer he took a job as a deckhand on a riverboat, but he quit and went back to the village. He never worked for cash again and never left Alaska. John married, and he and his wife, Elsie, lived in a small cabin and practiced a survivalist lifestyle. He hunted and covered a twenty-eight-mile circuit on foot every day to check his animal traps. Even after snowmobiles became available, he still hunted on snowshoes. When he and Elsie decided to settle in the village of Minto, Alaska, John became chief.

During the debate over land claims, his tribe asked John to testify at hearings in Fairbanks and Juneau, Alaska. His knowledge of the area enabled him to describe the traditional Native uses of hundreds of sites, including hunting and fishing areas and even battlegrounds from long-ago wars. His powerful speaking style influenced governors and congressmen.

Enei grew up in Navajo County, which covers almost ten thousand square miles (just over sixteen thousand square kilometers) and has a population of almost 113,000 people. Her family is from a small community of about five hundred people on the Shonto reservation.

Enei's mother is from the Tohono O'odham Tribe and her father is from the Diné (Navajo). When Enei was a young girl, her Navajo grandparents didn't speak any English, and since she is not fluent in Navajo, language was a barrier between them. That did not stop Enei from learning the traditional Navajo ways, however. Her grandfather was a Navajo medicine man, or spiritual leader, and she went to traditional ceremonies with him.

Enei grew up climbing rocks and playing outside among the sandstone rock formations. While she was in grades one through six, her family moved around the reservation so her mother could find employment as a health-care provider. Enei's father is the well-known artist Shonto Begay. As kids, Enei and her siblings would go to art shows with their father and help set up his artwork. The family lived in Navajo National Monument for a few years, while her father was a park ranger there and her mother went to graduate school.

Enei attended high school in the reservation community of Kayenta, Arizona, a small town with a population of fewer than six thousand people. The town is near one of the largest coal strip-mining operations and abandoned uranium mines in the United States. (From 1994 to 2007, the US Environmental Protection Agency found 520 abandoned uranium mines throughout the Navajo reservation.)[1] The town has no traffic lights, and the commercial district is composed of two hotels and a main store. Enei's family lived in the coal company's trailer court because there was no other housing. Many of her friends' parents worked at the coal mine.

The small community had seven churches when Enei was growing up. She always felt people on the reservation were treated differently depending on which church they attended. To Enei it seemed as if a battle was being waged for people's souls. When she spoke to her parents about the various religions, her dad said, "Well let's go check out this particular religion today."

Enei attended many churches but decided none were for her. Once she invited a friend to come to a traditional Navajo ceremony, and he told her his religion would not allow it. Enei could not understand why the churches didn't allow people to attend traditional Navajo ceremonies. Furthermore, she was shocked to learn that people were not only told they could not attend traditional ceremonies, but they were also told that their church was the only "right" way. She observes, "Within the religions themselves, traditional Navajo ways seem to be incorporated, but they don't allow you to practice a Navajo ceremony."

High school student government provided the opportunity for Enei to discover her organizational and leadership skills. She was in charge of the homecoming parade, a large community event that featured one hundred floats from all over the reservation. She did a great job and realized, "I enjoy telling people what to do."

High school can be a difficult time when teens are confronted with choices about drugs and alcohol. Enei became involved in sports and ran track for her school instead of getting involved in the drug scene. She saw the consequences from drug and alcohol use all around her, and she decided she did not want them in her life. Her mom, who never drank, worked to help many women who suffered the effects of drugs and alcohol. Her mother started the first women's shelter on the reservation and was instrumental in opening women's shelters all over the reservation.

Enei had a good scholastic record and took advantage of her academic options. One opportunity was a six-week intensive math and science program at the prestigious Phillips Academy in Andover, Massachusetts. She attended the program during the summers of her freshman, sophomore, and junior years in high school.

Her hard work paid off when Enei graduated with straight As in 1996. She gave the graduation keynote speech and told her classmates: "You are going to fall. You are going to make mistakes in life, but you just have to get back up and keep going."

Because of Enei's strong academic performance, along with her participation in extracurricular activities and programs, many colleges were eager to have her. She decided to go to Stanford University in California. She started out as a biology major but decided to change her major to geological and environmental sciences.

Enei wanted to work with environmental issues in some way, and she used summer internships to explore this field. She learned about the Inter Tribal Council of Arizona.[2] She says, "I wanted to work with them, so I just went and asked if they had anything for me to do." Her proactive efforts also helped her secure internships with both the Navajo government and the US Environmental Protection Agency. This is how she describes her approach to getting internships: "Mostly I figured out where I wanted to go and contacted them directly. They didn't necessarily have internships available, but I just kind of butted my way in. You have to make opportunities yourself. Just like on the reservation, we have to make our own jobs ourselves."

At first Enei felt that Stanford was close to home. However, she began to realize how far away she was from her culture. She recalls, "The entire culture of Stanford is very different. People have their own cars. There was a lot of wealth." It grew harder for Enei to stay in California as she recognized the inequalities between her Native culture and the one at school. In fact, these realizations came to her while she was studying the problems that cause the inequalities.

Enei grew increasingly uneasy when she began to take environmental science courses, including petroleum engineering classes. In one of her first geology classes, the students were given a theoretical problem and asked to find suitable locations to store nuclear waste. The class was told to look at a map of the United States and pick five places that were geologically sound, taking into consideration factors such as earthquakes, floods, and human populations. After examining all the information, the class decided the best places for storing waste were under Native lands. But Enei, who received a D on her report, came to a different conclusion: "I just could not put any nuclear waste in those places. I ended up putting it all in Texas military installations."

Enei was finding it more and more frustrating to be away from her reservation. The summer before her senior year at Stanford, she got an internship near her home with a Hopi group called Black Mesa Trust. The group organized people to save the Navajo aquifer from depletion caused by mining operations. The Natural Resources Defense Council[3] published a report showing depleted water levels under Black Mesa, home to the Hopi and Navajo, and the site of the Peabody Coal strip mine. The mine was pumping 3.1 million gallons of water from the underground Navajo aquifer each day, causing a severe decline in the amount of drinkable water. People back on the reservation were starting to protest, and leaders were trying to get people to become more aware about the coal mining operations there.

Through her work with the Black Mesa Trust, Enei helped inform people on the Hopi and Navajo reservations about the water decrease. She also organized a trip to Phoenix for a group from the Hopi Nation to take letters to the regional Bureau of Indian Affairs in protest. Enei remembers, "At the time, there were not many young people. I was doing a lot of the work, mostly with older Hopi men and older Navajo people."

In the fall, Enei returned to Stanford. Midway through her senior year, she made an important decision: "I had gone through a summer organizing and feeling like we were creating change, but when I got back to Stanford I was feeling as though I was studying all the time while surrounded by inequality. It was hard, and I dropped out of Stanford one semester before I was supposed to graduate. It was not something my parents were very happy about. But I was getting very upset with the institution and the fact that people put more weight on an education that comes from an institution than on an education that comes from tradition."

After she dropped out, the work she had done over the summer with the Black Mesa Trust was foremost in her mind. She was excited to learn that Chicano, Hopi, and Navajo students at Northern Arizona University had started a group called the Black Mesa Water Coalition. Enei started working with the group, whose goal was to stop Peabody Coal Company from mining on Black Mesa. Working together in the coali-

Enei Begaye

tion were Navajo and Hopi young people, despite the fact that there were hard feelings between the two tribes.

Trouble between the Navajo and the Hopi began in 1964, when the Navajo signed a contract with Peabody Coal allowing the company to use the Navajo water supply for their mining operations.[4] Two years later, the Hopi entered into a similar contract. The situation between the two tribes was exploited by Bechtel Corporation, the largest engineering company in the United States, and by Peabody Coal, the largest private coal company in the world. Peabody Coal needed the cheap Black Mesa coal to fuel two Bechtel Corporation power plants, the Mohave Generating Station and the Navajo Generating Station. The big question was what to do with the twelve thousand Navajo living on top of the coal deposits.

A lawyer named John Boyden, who was publicly representing some Hopi while secretly on the payroll of Peabody
Coal, went to Congress with a plan that gave almost one million acres of Black Mesa to the Hopi who lived far away from
the strip mining. The plan established the Navajo who were
living on Black Mesa as "trespassers" who could be relocated at government expense. A public relations firm was hired
to frame the situation as a phony range war between cattle-
herding Hopi and sheep-herding Navajo. Congress passed
the resulting law in 1974. There was no provision for a place
to put the relocated Navajo, but that was of no concern to
Bechtel Corporation or Peabody Coal. (Read more about the
relocation act in chapter 9.)

The Navajo got a poor reception when they went to the US
Congress to complain. By that time, Peabody Coal had what
they wanted, and Bechtel had their people entrenched in gov-
ernment positions in Washington. Bechtel's former president,
George Schultz, was secretary of state; its top lawyer, Caspar
Weinberger, was secretary of defense; and former director of
Bechtel Nuclear, Ken Davis, was deputy secretary of energy.
The president of Peabody Coal served on President Reagan's
Energy Advisory Board. To top it off, the Utah congressman
who introduced the final Navajo relocation legislation, Wayne
Owens, went to work in John Boyden's law firm when he lost
his bid for re-election.

More than thirty years later, Navajo resentment over the
relocation still existed. These long-standing hard feelings
presented challenges for the Black Mesa Water Coalition.
The coalition stressed that the mining affects both Hopi and
Navajo. Still, as Enei recalls, distrust ran deep: "We kept
on going because we had built good friendships with each
other. We realized a lot of the distrust came from the mining
operation. A lot of the bad feelings were because of what the
tribal governments were doing and the federal government
was doing, not necessarily what our neighbors and friends

were doing. I remember one of the big victories we had was shutting down some tribal government proposals to build a power plant on Black Mesa. We were able to do it because we had community meetings where the same people who were yelling at us not to trust the Hopis stood up and addressed the Hopi council people as 'brothers and sisters.' I think the coalition was able to create that alliance because we didn't have the same emotional baggage. A lot of us didn't grow up in relocation families. We did not have that intense anger a lot of others have."

The organization continues its work today with an all-volunteer crew. Black Mesa Trust is a grassroots organization whose members attend rallies and use bullhorns to voice their message: "Stop the Mining on Black Mesa."

Looking at Black Mesa today, it is easy to see why the Black Mesa Trust is determined to stop the mining operations. The damage to the landscape from strip mining is

Aeriel photo of Black Mesa mining

clearly visible; the mining process itself contaminates the groundwater and reduces the pristine aquifer. Bechtel Corporation and Peabody Coal have grown rich from mining, while the Navajo have the lowest per-person income in North America. Enei asks, "What job do we have to do to put food on the tables for our families and still honor our history and our duty to this land?"

The coal from Black Mesa is used to generate electricity for Los Angeles, Las Vegas, and the cities of Arizona. The transmission lines cross the Navajo and Hopi reservations, where some people don't even have service. Enei says, "Look at the reservation today. We have had mining for thirty years on Black Mesa, and yet we still have people without electricity and running water. We are still a broken economy, and the mining has destroyed thousands of archeological sites."

When Enei and Evon were first married and lived in the Gwich'in community, Enei worked with the Black Mesa Water Coalition from her new home in Alaska. Enei explains, "It was funny, because Evon's village has very good Internet capability. His village is very remote and you can only get there by plane—there are no grocery stores—but the Internet is great. The Internet service on the reservation in Arizona is awful. You can't even get Internet at school sometimes. It was easier for me to work from Alaska than it would have been from Arizona. Globalization is amazing."

No matter where they live, Enei and Evon work as a team on environmental issues and find sustainable strategies for all Native people. Enei says, "The crux of the problem is that the majority of jobs available to Native people provide no dignity. The jobs are counter to our cultural and spiritual connections to the earth and force us, as Winona LaDuke (see chapter 2) says, to 'cannibalize our own mother in order to live.'"

Evon notes, "I used to think it was more about my family and my village and my people, but over the years I realized

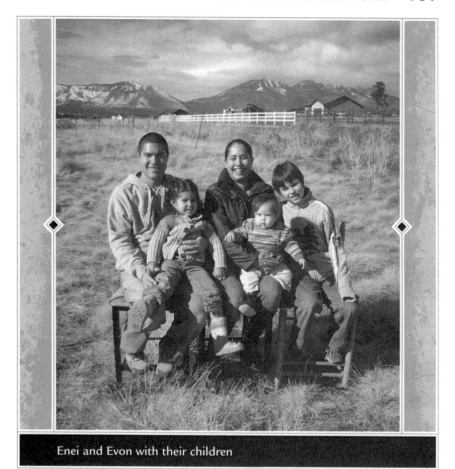

Enei and Evon with their children

how close we are as a larger, growing global community and how acts in my own small village may affect a village on the other side of the world. When we talk about being involved in any kind of change these days, it is almost inevitable the impact will be beyond our own communities."

Enei has advice for Native young folks: "Figure out what you like to do and what you can contribute to your community, whether it is urban or rural, and love it. It's not going to be easy. If you fall down, you have to keep picking yourself back up. Native kids don't get support sometimes. Read the statistics. People say you are not going to make it. We don't have to believe that. We can choose to be the statistic that is going to be in trouble and is not going to make it. That is an easy choice to make. We are surrounded a lot of times on the reservation by hopelessness. It gets passed down from generation to generation. However, we can choose not to be that statistic—we can work and make a different life for ourselves. It isn't easy.

"You don't necessarily have to be 'that good kid' all the time," she adds. "It is okay to react if there is injustice. It is okay to step out of line. Just make decisions you will be proud of, so you can look back and say, 'I would still do that and I would still make that decision if given a second chance.'"

Klee Benally

USES THE MEDIA TO EMPOWER NATIVE COMMUNITIES IN THEIR FIGHT FOR ENVIRONMENTAL JUSTICE

You might recognize Klee Benally as the lead vocalist and guitarist with Blackfire, the punk rock group whose double-disk CD, *Silence Is a Weapon,* was named the Native American Music Awards record of the year in 2008. Or you might know him because he has danced since childhood with the internationally known traditional Diné dance group, The Jones-Benally Family. But what you might not be aware of is that Klee began a media company to help communities take action to protect the environment. His company produces short documentaries and offers assistance and advice to people who are planning Indigenous media events. His films have been seen worldwide and have been used in the teaching curriculum at Northern Arizona University.

Klee is an enrolled member of the Diné (Navajo) Nation and currently lives in Flagstaff, Arizona. He was born in 1975 at Big Mountain on Black Mesa in Navajo County, Arizona, one year after Congress passed Public Law 93-531, a relocation act that forced twelve thousand Navajo to move from their homes and sacred sites. Bechtel Corporation and Peabody Coal Company sought the relocation

Klee Benally

because they needed the cheap and abundant coal found on Black Mesa to fuel Bechtel's two power plants. A public relations cover story invented by coal company lobbyists convinced many in Congress that the law's passage would settle a range war between the Hopi and Navajo. It was not revealed that the energy companies concocted the story to force the Navajo and their livestock off Black Mesa. Congress passed the relocation act, which was sponsored by

Senator John McCain in 1974, but the act did not give the Navajo people who were forced to move anywhere to live.[1] (Read more about the relocation act in chapter 8.) The relocation has caused more than thirty years of hard feelings between the Navajo and Hopi.

For Klee's family, the results of the new law were devastating. His parents and other relatives were living on land his family owned when the government installed a barbed wire fence that intersected one of his family's horse corrals, decreeing that one side was Navajo and the other side was Hopi. This fence cut their family off from their springs and grazing lands. Many of Klee's family members were told they were illegally occupying lands that were in fact their family's homeland. Even though Klee was a child, he remembers the anguish of the forced relocation: "I was raised in this. Some of my first memories were house meetings. I didn't really understand what was going on, but I began to realize something was not right when I saw the suffering of my elders. Grandfathers and grandmothers were crying and distressed. I saw families torn apart."

An important influence in Klee's upbringing was his grandmother, Roberta Blackgoat, who fought for Indigenous people's rights. She spoke out against the Peabody Coal Company and the relocation, and she defended the rights and culture of her tribe. Klee remembers following her around and learning from her when he was young. He believes she instilled in him a deep connection and respect for Mother Earth. Klee says his grandmother taught him to take care of the earth, ourselves, our families, and communities that embrace traditional cultural practices.

Social activism was always part of Klee's family life. Inside the cover of the Blackfire CD *One Nation Under* is a picture of three-year-old Klee in front of the relocation committee office holding a sign his parents made that reads "BIA Don't Kill Me." (BIA stands for Bureau of Indian Affairs, a United States government agency.) Klee and his siblings grew up attending meetings and court hearings with their parents on and off the reservation. The family also traveled to American Indian Movement (AIM) meetings and camps at the base of Big Mountain. As Klee remembers, "We were very young going to meetings. It wasn't a conscious effort of protecting Mother Earth. I felt like my brother, my sister, and I were born into this. Once you care deeply about something, it is hard not to take action when you see injustice."

Klee's sense of right and wrong is founded on a deep spiritual understanding. His father is a medicine man, and from childhood Klee participated in ceremonies that taught him to take care of the earth, to have reverence for creation, and to understand his sacred responsibilities. Klee explains, "If you do not take care of the land, it is not going to take care of you. You have to have a relationship with the land through prayers. Those prayers and offerings nurture you, but you also have to take care of the land so it will continue to nurture and sustain you."

Music is a big part of Klee's life. From a young age, he and his two siblings were immersed in Native singing and dancing. Their interest in music continued to develop over time. Klee's sister, Jeneda, was thirteen when she started playing the bass. His brother, Clayson, was ten when he took up the drums. Klee was twelve years old when he picked up the guitar. The three siblings played and practiced together as a group. They got their first show in 1990 when they were asked to perform at a New Year's Eve party. The crowd went wild for the Native punk rock band, and Blackfire was born.

Since that fateful night, the band's popularity has grown. Blackfire has toured throughout the United States and Europe. Their CD, *One Nation Under*, was named the Native American Music Awards best rock recording in 2002. The group has gone on to win numerous awards.

Social justice is always a message in Klee's music and a goal in his life, so he decided to use his knowledge of music production to make documentary films about social and

Klee Benally with the Jones-Benally Family

environmental issues. In 2001 Klee produced his first documentary, a short film titled *Crisis on Black Mesa*. The film
examines how the strip mine affected the Native people living
on Black Mesa and the disastrous effects it has had on the
environment. From this experience, Klee learned that film
can be an important tool to educate people and give a voice
to those who are hurt by the actions of the government and
powerful energy companies. Klee wanted to alert the public
about corporate disregard for the environment and human
lives, so in August 2001 he founded Indigenous Action Media,
which is still operating today.

A documentary film Klee produced in 2005, *The Snowbowl Effect*, exposes the disregard and disrespect for Native
people that made the development of the Snowbowl Ski
Resort in Flagstaff, Arizona, possible. In 1938, during the
Great Depression, the US Forest Service permitted the building of the ski resort on San Francisco Peaks, one of the four
Navajo Sacred Mountains. The mountains are sacred to more
than thirteen Native tribes. As Klee's grandmother Roberta
Blackgoat explained, "Between these four Sacred Mountains
is a room for the Diné people, where it has been made like a

church, and way out on the west side, by the San Francisco Peaks, inside the room is our altar." The Snowbowl Ski Resort sits on that altar.

The US Forest Service ignored the fact that the mountain was sacred to the Navajo when the resort was first built and continued to insult the Navajo people as the resort expanded over time. In 1960 the resort corporation proposed more development, which Native communities fiercely resisted. Their concerns and needs were ignored. Then again, in 1983, the Snowbowl Ski Resort was allowed to develop into new areas. The continued expansion essentially defined Indigenous sacred rights as unimportant.

The Navajo's holy San Francisco Peaks faced another assault in 1997, when plans for increased development and expansion of the resort were made public. When one of Klee's friends contacted him about the proposed expansion, Klee knew he had to kick into gear since the resort plans were moving fast.

A week before Thanksgiving, Klee, his brother, and a cousin drove to the ski resort to gather some facts. What they learned at the lodge was shocking. The resort company was pushing the proposed expansion of the ski area on the sacred peaks, yet only one meeting for public comment was being held. The three young men also learned there had been no outreach to any of the affected communities, and the resort corporation was basing the new development on an outdated environmental impact statement from 1979.

Klee attended the public meeting and voiced his concerns. "This is a scam!" he told the other attendees. He pointed out the need for a well-publicized public meeting. He knew the lack of public information was intentional; the resort was trying to push through development without consulting the Native communities. The developers knew that the Native people would not approve. Klee also pointed out that the resort corporation was using an environmental impact statement from 1979 and that a current one was needed.

Native people who consider San Francisco Peaks sacred and non-Native people who want to develop the land have very different points of view. Non-Native people see the land as a source of money and lighthearted fun. Says Klee, "Just trying to talk to and educate people is a challenge. I've been offering prayers on this holy mountain and a ski resort manager asked me to leave. Other people were telling me, 'You are on the wrong side of the mountain; you Indians don't belong here.' That is just within the last couple of years! It is unfortunate in this day and age. But fortunately, in this community and in other communities, people have really stepped up and recognized the injustices we are still facing. This is an issue that doesn't just affect us as Native people—it affects many people. As we fight to protect our sacred sites, we are forced to justify our religious beliefs as being valid to a system that does not really view them that way."

The needs and concerns of the Native community are again being ignored as expansion of Snowbowl Ski Resort

Klee Benally

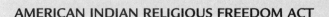

AMERICAN INDIAN RELIGIOUS FREEDOM ACT

The American Indian Religious Freedom Act was passed in 1978 to protect and preserve the traditional religious rights and cultural practices of Native people in the United States. This includes access to sacred sites, freedom to worship through ceremonial and traditional rights, and use and possession of sacred objects.

continues. In a new affront to Native people, the resort is now using "reclaimed" sewage water from Flagstaff to create artificial snow for holiday skiers. Klee makes this comparison: "It would be akin to spraying sewage on a holy shrine or church or destroying part of the Vatican and converting it to a skateboard park."

The Hopi's and Navajo's attempts to use the American Indian Religious Freedom Act of 1978 to stop the resort's expansions and spraying of wastewater have lost in federal courts, but the struggle is not over for Klee. He says, "My involvement with the holy San Francisco Peaks continues to this day."

Klee and his coworkers at Indigenous Action Media have produced their third documentary, *Making a Stand at Desert Rock*. It tells the story of people who are trying to protect the land by stopping the construction of the coal-fired Desert Rock power plant that Sithe Global Power proposes to build on Navajo Reservation Four Corners land. After the power plant is built, each year it will emit 12.7 million tons of carbon dioxide into the atmosphere. Carbon dioxide is a major contributor to climate change.

In 2004 Klee created a group called Outta Your Backpack Media to empower Indigenous youth to tell their stories using media equipment that can be carried in a backpack. Klee believes that everything a person needs to become a filmmaker or news outlet is completely available: "With social networking services, and with any computer today, you can make a video with freely available software. From cell phones to digital still cameras to very accessible video cameras, with just those minimal resources, young people can create a media center out of their backpacks. Our structure has no hierarchy. We don't believe in bosses—we believe in collective power."

Outta Your Backpack Media reaches out to Indigenous youth who are experiencing both environmental and cultural crises. The group offers consultation, and its members travel and conduct workshops with young people. The workshops include a specific lesson explaining media justice. Participants are asked to define the most pressing issues they care about and look for solutions and actions. The workshops help young people recognize the power within their own community.

Empowerment of individuals and the community are the goals of Klee's work. He does not like to be called an activist because, in his opinion, the term separates him from his community. Rather than creating a powerful organization that has political influence, he is interested in supporting and creating power that a community can use. He believes strongly in the value of an empowered community. As Klee explains, "When you have community power or empowered youth—that is life changing."

Klee believes the lack of power that many Native youth experience is the failure of the schools they attend. He explains that in public schools there are no teaching materials that support the values of Indigenous people. Native children do not read the true history of their people; they read only about the great Native chiefs who were defeated by the white man. Klee states, "History is written by the victors of war, the conquerors in this case. We have always had to struggle, and we have always known that our identity is something more than that."

Klee believes serious thought and investigation are required to grasp the current situation of Indigenous people. He asserts, "There needs to be an understanding of how complicated and how sophisticated the oppression of Native people is today." In spite of the granting of some civil rights, tribes are being denied or stripped of their federal status. There have been abuses to their sacred sites and burial mounds. Indigenous communities are being divided between the United States and Mexico. Years ago Roberta Blackgoat lamented, "Not just the Navajos are suffering, it's all Indians living in Indian country who are suffering."

Klee stresses the point: "We are, as Indigenous peoples, still paying the price of energy consumption of the dominant society. The greater and more dominant culture needs to come to terms with environmental racism and the suffering it causes. Uranium mines, coal-fired power plants, nuclear waste facilities, nuclear power plants, and border walls— the suffering that is caused by those things will never be addressed until the dominant society understands that suffering and feels that suffering."

It is a safe assumption that all of the many projects that Klee Benally is working on will benefit Native people as well as their environment. His integrity and commitment to his goals are reflected in this statement: "I'm just an individual facilitating actions. I want the real connection to be between the readers of this book and the issues within their communities."

Teague Allston

WORKS FOR ENVIRONMENTAL JUSTICE AND ENSURES A TRIBAL VOICE IS HEARD IN WASHINGTON, DC

hough still in his early twenties, Teague Allston is already working for environmental justice in the National Wildlife Federation (NWF) Tribal Lands Program. His work with tribes includes developing habitat and wildlife management projects, but his primary focus is shaping climate and energy policies. As he describes it, "I fight to ensure a tribal voice is heard in Washington, DC."

Teague was born in Columbia, South Carolina, on August 12, 1987. When he was growing up, his family split their time between their home in South Carolina and their farm in Southampton County, Virginia, the ancestral home of the Nottoway Tribe.

Teague Allston

Teague Allston as a child

Teague's mother, Lynette Allston, is chief and tribal council chairman of the Nottoway Indian Tribe of Virginia, and she is active within the larger Native community in Virginia. Teague describes his mother as a very strong-willed woman who is well respected in her community. Lynette always believed Teague was meant to be an environmentalist. She recalls, "When Teague was little, about five or six, he played soccer. During practice or even in the middle of a game, all of the little kids would run as a pack. All of these kids would be at the other end of the field, but Teague would be bending down looking in the grass, following a bug, fooling with a clump of grass, or looking at a leaf."

Teague's father, Allard Allston, is a Virginia attorney and legal counsel for the Nottoway Indian Tribe. His father's accomplishments have been an inspiration to Teague, who has always wanted to live up to his father's example of integrity.

Because Teague's father is an African American and his mother is a Native American, his parents wanted him to understand the struggles of both groups of ancestors. His biracial background helped him to appreciate the similarities and differences between his parents' cultures. His mother taught him about the third-class status Indians were given in Virginia and how every effort was made to destroy their Native heritage. To teach him about his African American roots, his parents took him to visit the former rice plantation where his father's ancestors were slaves. These and other lessons gave Teague an appreciation for the opportunities he has in life. He also gained an understanding of the example he must set for future generations.

Teague went to school in South Carolina, but every weekend and holiday, his family drove to Virginia. It was during these visits to the farm that his interest in nature and science began to take hold. He spent almost every waking moment outside, wandering in the woods, climbing trees, looking at insects, and just generally getting dirty. He was a curious kid who was always fascinated by the ways living things interacted with each other. Because he was exploring the same places his ancestors had occupied for centuries, Teague felt a deep sense of belonging and a unique connection to the land.

When Teague was growing up, his family attended powwows and spiritual gatherings. Teague remembers feeling that those were the only times he was surrounded by people who were just like him. His favorite part of a powwow came at the end, after most of the visitors had left and the sun was starting to go down. This was the time when tribal members, dancers, and folks from other local tribes would gather around the drums for the final song. Being part of these small groups and sharing these deeply spiritual moments strengthened Teague's sense of community and place within his tribe.

School was extremely important in the Allston family; Teague's parents believed education was critical to their son's empowerment. His parents' encouragement nourished his love of learning. Teague did well from elementary school through high school, and he received academic honors from his school district.

Navigating school as a minority posed special challenges for Teague. South Carolina doesn't have a large Native population, and there weren't any other Native students in his school. Because Teague is biracial, people asked him about his ethnicity on a daily basis. When he told them he was half Native, people would sometimes ask him stereotypical

Teague Allston with his mother

questions, such as "Do you have a tepee?" He found it difficult to explain his Native heritage. He recalls, "I experienced
cultural ignorance more than anything. People would tell me
their 'grandmother was a Cherokee princess' or ask me to
take them on a vision quest and things like that."

Teague's teenage years were a time of growth and transition. Decisions made during this period can influence a
person's course in life, and this was true for Teague. Even
though he was around other teens who were making bad
choices, Teague was raised to be responsible and he tried to

keep to that path. Although there was a period during which he was a rebellious teenager who was bored with his rural lifestyle, he was still able to stay focused on what he wanted to accomplish in his life.

Teague always knew he would go to college, and Duke University in Durham, North Carolina, was his first choice. College exposed Teague to the world outside the one he grew up in. For the first time he was meeting people from different cultures and walks of life, and Teague learned as much from his peers as he did from his teachers. He regained the curiosity he felt he had lost in high school. The university provided an environment where he felt comfortable pursuing his own interests, even though he sometimes felt frustrated when his college textbooks gave the impression that Native people did not exist anymore.

During his final year of college he signed up for a course in environmental science. As it turned out, the course had a direct influence on Teague's career plans. The class was taught almost entirely outdoors, and the students spent hours in the forest learning how to conduct field research. The course reminded Teague of the countless days he had spent as a child looking at insects and leaves. The course focused on understanding the interactions between species in an ecosystem and on the effects of land development that does not respect those interactions. Teague saw a connection between studying the environment and his personal connection with the natural world. He was determined to find meaningful work that he loved with a career in the field of environmental science. He wanted to relate his Native American upbringing to his connection with the land.

After Teague graduated from college, he went to work as a research intern at the world's largest living history museum, Colonial Williamsburg in Virginia. He dug up firsthand accounts of the interactions between early colonists and local tribes, including his own. It was an engaging job, but Teague was not an archeologist. Instead, he wanted work that had an environmental focus. He was looking in the classified ads in the back of *Indian Country Today* when he saw a job posting for a national tribal and public lands stewardship intern. It was a one-year position at the NWF that combined environmental science and Native American issues and policies. This was more like it! He applied, had an interview, and was accepted for the position. Teague packed up his belongings and moved to Colorado, excited to work for the NWF's Tribal Lands Conservation Program.

In Colorado, Teague began his internship working on a program called "The New Energy Future in Indian Country: Confronting Climate Change, Creating Jobs, and Conserving Nature." For one of his first tasks, he used skills he learned in college to compose a report about the renewable energy sources available on tribal land. The report included information from a 2009 study by the Bureau of Indian Affairs that identified seventy-seven reservations that could support viable wind-based economies and information from a Natural Renewable Energy Laboratory report that stated tribal lands alone could meet 14 percent of the nation's energy needs. Teague also included information he learned from tribal members about the legal and financial obstacles that make it difficult for most tribes to take advantage of renewable energy sources.

Teague is enthusiastic about the huge push for wind and solar power nationwide, especially on tribal lands. He knows there is financial interest. However, tribal sovereignty can make it hard for nontribal entities to make investments on Native land. Tribes are not given the same tax credits that are available to states. By working on this and other issues, Teague hopes to bring numerous energy-related jobs to reservations with struggling economies.

Teague believes Native Americans and First Nations people are uniquely situated to bring about great changes in energy policy, but their voices need to be heard. He understands that

Indigenous people are generally recognized as the original stewards of the land, but he also knows that many people aren't even aware of a specific tribe's existence or its stand on an energy issue. Sometimes tribes seem almost invisible to the general public. Teague sees reversing this invisibility as critical. He explains, "We have to get people to appeal to their representatives or senators or congress people to tell them, 'Yes, we are here. This is what we want.'"

Education for Teague is an ongoing process. He plans to pursue a law degree and use the law to block unsustainable environmental development. His hope is to influence future policies that promote sustainable development and protect habitat diversity by pushing for stricter regulation of the gas, mining, and oil industries, which all manage to skirt the laws on a regular basis. He intends to advocate for

Teague Allston

NOTTOWAY INDIAN TRIBE OF VIRGINIA

In February 2010, the Nottoway and the Powhatan Patawomeck Indian Tribes were finally able to celebrate tribal recognition by the commonwealth of Virginia, ending a twenty-one-year battle between the state and the tribes. Chief Lynette Allston, Teague's mother and chief of the Nottoway Indian Tribe, was elated by the long-awaited decision. The Virginia state house and senate committee members heard her testimony for recognition along with that of legendary entertainment personality Wayne Newton, who testified on the behalf of his tribe, the Powhatan Patawomecks.

legislation that increases government funding to tribes for conservation and renewable energy development.

Young folks who want to change the world and protect the natural order would do well to follow Teague's advice: "Start by listening to your elders and embracing your traditions. The relationship between humans and the natural world has always been a cornerstone of Native life. Native Americans are the original environmentalists. Our people were practicing sustainability long before it became a catchphrase."

When Teague speaks with kids who are budding environmentalists, he tells them to get involved with other people who share their goals. He suggests that they ask their parents to start recycling at home or convince their principal to start a schoolyard garden or put up a bird feeder. He reminds students that even small projects can go a long way toward influencing other people, including their parents, teachers, friends, and neighbors. He urges, "Go to the library and start reading about the plants and wildlife in your own backyard. Learn about ecosystems and how things interact in nature."

Teague offers good advice based on personal experience: "Spend time outside. People are spending most of their time inside watching TV, cruising the Internet, and playing video games. There's nothing wrong with any of these activities in moderation, but we weren't designed to spend our days sitting down and staring at a screen. It's bad for our health and has a way of disconnecting us from the real world. Go outside, and take your friends with you. There's no better way to convince people of what's at stake than by taking them outside and showing them firsthand."

Aboriginal Youth Initiative
Email: careers@nextgen.org

Arctic National Wildlife Refuge
arctic.fws.gov

Blackfire
Attention: Klee Benally
PO Box 1492
Flagstaff, AZ 86002
blackfire.net

Black Mesa Water Coalition
PO Box 613
Flagstaff, AZ 86002
Phone: 928-213-5909
blackmesawatercoalition.org

Canadian Indigenous
Tar Sands Campaign
180 Metcalfe Street, Suite 500
Ottawa, ON
Canada K2P 1P5
Phone: 613-237-1717, ext. 106
Twitter: @claytonIEN

The Center for Food Safety
660 Pennsylvania Avenue SE,
Suite 302
Washington, DC 20003
Phone: 202-547-9359
Fax: 202-547-9429
office@centerforfoodsafety.org
centerforfoodsafety.org

Defenders of the Land
575 Palmerston Avenue
Toronto, ON
Canada M6G 2P6
defendersoftheland.org

Defenders of Wildlife
1130 17th Street NW
Washington, DC 20036
Phone: 800-385-9712
defenders.org

Greenpeace Canada
33 Cecil Street
Toronto, ON
Canada M5T 1N1
Phone: 416-597-8408
Toll-free: 800-320-7183
Fax: 416-597-8422
greenpeace.org/canada

Greenpeace USA
702 H Street NW, Suite 300
Washington, DC 20001
Phone: 202-462-1177
greenpeace.org/usa

Gwich'in Steering Committee
122 First Avenue, Box 2
Fairbanks, AK 99701
Phone: 907-458-8264
Fax: 907-457-8265
gwichinsteeringcommittee.org

Honor the Earth
2104 Stevens Avenue South
Minneapolis, MN 55404
Phone: 612-879-7529
honorearth.org

Independent Indigenous Media
PO Box 1492
Flagstaff, AZ 86004
Phone: 928-527-1431
(Taala Hooghan Infoshop)
indigenousaction.org

Indigenous Environmental Network
PO Box 485
Bemidji, MN 56619
Phone: 218-751-4967
ienearth.org

The Indigenous Leadership Institute
409 College Road, Suite 3
Fairbanks, AK 99701
Phone: 907-374-5950
indigenousleadership.org

National Environmental Coalition
of Native Americans
necona.indigenousnative.org

National Wildlife Federation
11100 Wildlife Center Drive
Reston, VA 20190
Phone: 800-822-9919
nwf.org

CAREERS: The Next Generation
10787 180th Street NW, Suite 200
Edmonton, AB
Canada T5S 1G6
Phone: 780-426-3414
Toll-free in Canada: 888-757-7172
Fax: 780-428-8164
nextgen.org

Noam Chomsky
chomsky.info

Outta Your Backpack Media
1700 N. 2nd Street
Flagstaff, AZ 86004
oybm.org

Save Our Rice Alliance
PO Box 1528
Bemidji, MN 56619
Phone: 218-368-5050
saveourrice.org

Shonto Begay
shontogallery.com

Trees, Water, & People
633 Remington Street
Ft. Collins, CO 80524
Phone: 970-484-3678
Toll-free: 877-606-4897
treeswaterpeople.org

US Department of Energy—
Tribal Energy Program
apps1.eere.energy.gov/tribalenergy

Water is Life—No Snowmaking

truesnow.org

White Earth Land Recovery Project

607 Main Avenue

Callaway, MN 56521

welrp.org

Wolfman Jack

radiohof.org/discjockey/wolfman
jack.html

YES!

240 Harkleroad Avenue

Santa Cruz, CA 95062

Phone: 831-465-1091

yesworld.org

Chapter 1

1. Song, Vivian. 2011. "Rare Cancer Strikes." *Oil and Sand*. Accessed April 1. oilsandstruth.org/rare-cancer-strikes.

Chapter 2

1. Leonard, Christopher. 2009. "Monsanto Squeezes Out Seed Business Competition, AP Investigation Finds." *Huffpost Business*, Accessed December 13. huffingtonpost.com.
2. Center for Food Safety. 2011. "Corporate Control and Seed Monopolies." Accessed April 15. centerforfoodsafety.org.

Chapter 4

1. US Environmental Protection Agency. 2011. "Climate Change Basic Information." Accessed April 15. epa.gov/climatechange/basicinfo.html.

Chapter 8

1. US Environmental Protection Agency. 2010. "Addressing Uranium Contamination in the Navajo Nation." epa.gov/region9/superfund/navajo-nation/abandoned-uranium.html.
2. Inter Tribal Council of Arizona. itcaonline.com.
3. Natural Resources Defense Council. 2006. "Drinking Water Jeopardized in Arizona's Black Mesa Region." nrdc.org.
4. "Black Mesa Peabody Coal Controversy." Wikipedia, last modified May 6, 2011. wikipedia.org/wiki/Black_Mesa_Peabody_Coal_controversy.

Chapter 9

1. University of Colorado at Boulder. "Deep Background." Accessed April 18, 2011. colorado.edu/studentgroups/tsc/deep.html.

Vincent Schilling is a member of the Saint Regis Mohawk Tribe and an award-winning author, journalist, and professional photographer. He is also the host of the award-winning blog talk radio show Native Trailblazers (blogtalkradio.com/NativeTrailblazers).

Vincent has contributed to the leading Native American news publication in the United States, *Indian Country Today*, and to other Native publications, such as *Native Times, Tribal College Journal,* and *Winds of Change.* He also is a contributor to *Arthritis Today, Children's Digest, Inside Business, Tidewater Parent,* and *The Virginian-Pilot.*

His first book, *Native Athletes in Action,* won distinction with a Moonbeam Children's Book Award in multicultural nonfiction and acclaim as book of the month from *Native America Calling,* a nationally syndicated Native American radio show. He released his second book, *Native Men of Courage,* in the summer of 2008.

His most recent book for children, *Native Musicians in the Groove,* is about Native musicians and vocal artists. The book was a finalist in the 2010 Next Generation Indie Book Awards and also won the Moonbeam Children's Book Award in multicultural nonfiction.

Vincent lives in Virginia Beach, Virginia, with his wife, Delores. In their travels around the country, Vincent has been fortunate to share his experiences with Native youth as far away as Ronan, Montana.

Vincent can be contacted via his Twitter address, @Native trailblaz. To see some of his photos, visit vincent schilling portfolio.shutterfly.com.

Vincent Schilling

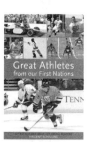

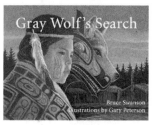